HR APPROVED WAYS TO TELL EMPLOYEES ANYTHING - BOOK 1 PERFORMANCE & COMPETENCE EDITION

SMART HR-APPROVED PHRASES FOR MANAGERS WHO KNOW THERE'S NO SUCH THING AS A STUPID EMPLOYEE—COMMUNICATION & COACHING FOR DIFFICULT WORKPLACE CONVERSATIONS

S.R. BROWN

HALCYON ENTERPRISE INC.

Disclaimer Notice:

This book is a communication guide, not legal advice, HR policy guidance, or a substitute for professional counsel.

This is a phrase reference for workplace conversations with practical language suggestions for difficult situations. This is NOT legal advice, HR policy, documentation templates, compliance guidance, or a guarantee against liability.

Consult your HR department and legal counsel before taking serious employment actions like termination, formal discipline, or addressing potential discrimination claims. Follow your organization's policies and documentation requirements. Understand relevant employment laws in your jurisdiction.

Critical situations requiring professional guidance include terminations or formal performance improvement plans, potential discrimination or harassment claims, issues involving protected classes or ADA accommodations, situations where an employee threatens legal action, and any time you're unsure about legal implications.

Employment laws vary by location, industry, and company size. What works in one workplace may not work in another. This book provides better words for difficult conversations. It doesn't replace good judgment, organizational policy, HR expertise, or legal counsel.

By using this book, you acknowledge that you're responsible for following your organization's policies, complying with applicable laws, seeking appropriate professional guidance, and adapting communication to your specific circumstances. The author and publisher assume no liability for employment decisions or their outcomes.

Think of it this way: This book is your communication toolkit. Your HR department and legal counsel are your safety net. Use both.

Paperback ISBN: 979-8-9927679-4-0

INTRODUCTION

You're staring at subpar work. Again. And you're mentally rehearsing the conversation you need to have. Again.

The problem isn't that you don't know there's a problem. The problem is you don't know what to say that'll break through to fix it and get the results you need from the offending team member.

That's where this book comes in. That's the gap this book fills.

THE PROBLEM WITH MOST FEEDBACK

Most managers know what they're thinking when an employee's performance falls short. The problem is translating that thought into professional language that actually communicates the issue and drives improvement.

What you're thinking: "This is terrible." **What you usually say:** "There are some areas for improvement here." **What happens:** Nothing changes because you weren't clear enough.

Or worse:

What you're thinking: "Why does this take you so long?" **What you actually say:** "What obstacles are slowing you down?" **What happens:** HR conversation, defensive employee, and you're managing a situation instead of performance.

You need language that lives in the middle—clear enough that the message lands, professional enough that you stay out of trouble.

WHAT THIS BOOK ACTUALLY IS

This is a phrase reference guide containing 573 professional alternatives for difficult performance conversations. It gives you the exact words to use when you need to tell an employee their work is subpar, their productivity is low, they're not understanding something, they can't manage time, or they lack basic initiative.

This book contains:

- Over 570 HR-appropriate phrases for addressing performance issues
- Real workplace scenarios with multiple response options (diplomatic to firm)
- Translation examples: "What You're Thinking" → "What You Should Say"
- Specific scripts you can adapt and use immediately
- Quick reference boxes for fast access to essential phrases

This book does NOT contain:

- HR policy guidance or legal advice
- Performance improvement plan templates
- Documentation procedures or termination guidance
- General management theory or leadership development concepts

This isn't about becoming a better manager overall. It's about having the right words for specific, difficult conversations.

WHY STANDARD ADVICE DOESN'T WORK

Generic communication advice tends to fail in two ways:

Too Vague: "Let's discuss areas for growth" tells an employee nothing specific enough to change. Three months later, you're having the same conversation because they had no idea what you actually meant.

Too Blunt: "You're not capable of this role" might be accurate, but it's language that creates problems rather than solving them.

You need phrases that are **direct enough to create change, professional enough to keep you out of trouble.** That's what the over 570 phrases in this book provide.

HOW THIS BOOK WORKS

The chapters cover the most common performance conversations managers face:

- **When Work Quality Is Below Standard** — Addressing subpar work without saying "this is garbage"
- **Addressing Slow Workers & Low Productivity** — Handling speed and output issues without accusations
- **When They Don't Get It (Comprehension Issues)** — Addressing understanding gaps without questioning intelligence
- **Missed Deadlines & Poor Time Management** — Requiring timely delivery without unreasonable pressure
- **Lack of Initiative & Passive Work Styles** — Expecting proactive work without overreach

Each chapter follows the same structure:

1. **Real Talk:** Honest acknowledgment of the actual problem
2. **Key Communication Principles:** Practical tips for these conversations

3. **Let's Get Real Scenarios:** Specific situations with multiple phrasing options
4. **HR-Approved Phrase Collection:** 60-100+ alternatives organized by situation
5. **Quick Reference Box:** 10 essential go-to phrases

Read cover to cover or jump to the chapter you need right now. Each chapter stands alone.

THE CORE PHILOSOPHY

This book operates on one belief: **Clarity without cruelty is possible—and necessary.**

Letting someone believe everything is fine when it isn't doesn't help them. But clarity doesn't require brutality. The phrases in this book help you find language that:

- Identifies the specific problem
- Sets clear expectations for improvement
- Maintains professional standards
- Creates accountability without personal attacks

WHEN TO USE THIS BOOK

Use this book when you're about to have a conversation where:

- You need to address a performance or capability problem
- You know what you're thinking, but not how to say it professionally
- You want to be direct without damaging the relationship
- You need the conversation to actually drive change

Flip to the relevant chapter. Find the scenario closest to yours. Use or adapt the phrases. Have the conversation. Please read the disclaimer at the beginning of this book.

INTRODUCTION

The words matter. This book gives you 573 of the right ones.

ONE
WHEN WORK QUALITY IS BELOW STANDARD

"This Needs Improvement"
(Translation: This Is Terrible)

Real Talk

Let's not dance around it: sometimes the work you get back is just bad. Not "needs a few tweaks" bad. Not "let's adjust the approach" bad. Bad bad. The kind of bad that makes you wonder if the person actually read the assignment, understood their job description, or possesses basic reasoning skills.

Maybe it's a report that reads like it was written by someone who's never seen a report before. Maybe it's a presentation that somehow misses the entire point of the project. Maybe it's work so riddled with errors that you'd actually save time doing it yourself from scratch. And here's the kicker: they often turn it in with complete confidence, as if they've just handed you gold.

Saying "this is terrible," or "did you even try?" or "are you sure you're qualified for this job?" probably isn't your best move. But you also can't let substandard work slide, because it reflects on you, your team, and ultimately affects actual business outcomes. This chapter gives you the words to communicate that the work is unacceptable without using language that could get you in trouble.

Five Principles for the 'Your Work Isn't Good Enough' Conversation

- **Be specific, not sweeping.** Instead of "this whole thing is wrong," identify concrete gaps: "The data analysis section doesn't address the three key metrics we discussed."

- **Separate effort from outcome.** "You didn't try hard enough" isn't going to help anyone. Focus on results: "The final deliverable doesn't meet the standards we need for client presentations."

- **Ask diagnostic questions first.** Sometimes work is bad because of miscommunication, unclear expectations, or a lack of resources. Start with "walk me through your process" before concluding they're just incompetent.

- **Show, don't just tell.** When work fundamentally misses the mark, an example of what "good" looks like is worth a thousand corrections. Just don't frame it as "see how easy this is?"

- **Scale your directness to the situation.** First offense with a new task? Start gently. Third report in a row that's unusable? Time to be more direct about the capability gap.

Let's Get Real Scenarios

Scenario 1: The Incomprehensible Report

Situation: An employee submitted a quarterly analysis that's so poorly organized and unclear that you can't actually extract any useful information from it. The data might be in there somewhere, but the presentation is a mess, the conclusions don't follow from the findings, and the executive summary somehow makes things more confusing.

What You're Thinking: "Were you somehow impaired while writing this? How did you think this was ready to submit? I literally cannot understand what you're trying to say, and I work in this field every day."

What You Should Say:

Diplomatic: "I'm having trouble following the flow of information in this report. Let's sit down together, and I'll walk you through the structure we need for this type of analysis. I want to make sure the key findings are clear and the recommendations are well-supported by the data."

- **What you're communicating:** "I can't understand your report. It's confusing and doesn't make sense. I'm going to show you how to do it the right way because you clearly don't know how."

Breaking it down:

- **"I'm having trouble following the flow of information"** = "Your report is confusing and jumps around too much."
- **"Let's sit down together and I'll walk you through the structure"** = "I'm going to teach you how to organize this properly because you didn't do it right."
- **"Key findings are clear"** = "The most important information should be easy to find and understand, but right now it's not."
- **"Recommendations are well-supported by the data"** = "When you tell people what they should do, you need to prove it with facts and numbers. You didn't do that."

More Direct: "This report isn't meeting the standard we need for executive review. The organization is unclear, the conclusions aren't supported by the analysis, and the key metrics are difficult to extract.

We need to restructure this completely. Let me show you a previous report that illustrates the format and level of clarity that's needed."

- **What you're communicating:** "This report isn't good enough to show to the executives. It's poorly organized, your conclusions don't match up with your facts, and I can't even find the important numbers. We basically have to redo the whole thing. I'll show you an old report that was done correctly so you can see what it's supposed to look like."

Breaking it down:

- **"Isn't meeting the standard we need for executive review"** = "This is too bad to show to the bosses"
- **"The organization is unclear"** = "This is all over the place and doesn't flow in a logical order"
- **"The conclusions aren't supported by the analysis"** = "You're making claims, but your data doesn't prove what you're saying is true"
- **"Key metrics are difficult to extract"** = "I can't easily find the important numbers and facts I need"
- **"We need to restructure this completely"** = "We have to rebuild this from scratch—it's not just a few fixes"
- **"Let me show you a previous report that illustrates the format and level of clarity that's needed"** = "I'm going to show you an example of a good report so you can copy that style and finally understand what you're supposed to be doing"

Firm: "This report does not work in its current form. The analysis is incomplete, the structure doesn't align with our standard format, and the conclusions aren't adequately supported. This needs significant rework before it's ready for review. I'm going to share our reporting template and two examples of acceptable work, and I need you to rebuild this using those as your guide."

- **What this means:** "This report is unacceptable and can't be used. You didn't finish analyzing everything you were supposed to, you didn't follow the format we always use, and you're making claims without enough proof. This needs major work before anyone can even look at it. I'm giving you our template and two examples of reports that were actually done right, and you need to start over and follow those exactly."

Breaking it down:

- **"Does not work in its current form"** = "This is completely unusable the way it is now"
- **"The analysis is incomplete"** = "You didn't finish the job—you left out important parts"
- **"Doesn't align with our standard format"** = "You didn't follow the template everyone is supposed to use. This looks totally different from how our reports should look"
- **"Conclusions aren't adequately supported"** = "You're not giving enough evidence to back up what you're saying"
- **"Needs significant rework before it's ready for review"** = "This needs so much work that no one should even read it until you fix it"
- **"I need you to rebuild this using those as your guide"** = "Start over from the beginning and copy the style and format of the good examples I'm giving you. Don't just make small changes —redo the whole thing."

Why This Works: You're clearly stating the work is unacceptable without saying "this is garbage." You're identifying specific problems (organization, clarity, support for conclusions) rather than making it about their intelligence or competence. The offer to show examples frames it as a learning opportunity while making it crystal clear that the current work doesn't cut it.

Scenario 2: They Think They Nailed It (But They Didn't)

Situation: An employee completed a project and clearly believes they did excellent work—they're proud, they may have even told others about it—but the reality is that they completely missed the point of the assignment. The deliverable technically addresses the surface-level request but demonstrates a fundamental misunderstanding of what was actually needed or why it mattered.

What You're Thinking: "You're so confident right now, and you have no idea how badly you missed the mark. This is like I asked for a financial projection and you gave me a grocery list. How are you this pleased with yourself?"

What You Should Say:

Diplomatic: "I can see you put work into this. I think there may have been some miscommunication about the project objectives, though. The deliverable you've created addresses [X], but what we actually needed was [Y]. Let's talk through the original request so we're aligned on the business goal behind this project."

What you're communicating: "You worked hard, but you did the wrong thing. We weren't on the same page about what this project was supposed to accomplish. You focused on the wrong stuff, and now we need to figure out what we actually need. Let me explain what the real goal was."

Breaking it down:

- **"I can see you put work into this"** = "I know you tried, and I'm acknowledging that before I tell you it's wrong"
- **"There may have been some miscommunication about the project objectives"** = "You misunderstood what this was supposed to be, but I'm being nice and saying maybe we both got confused"
- **"The deliverable you've created addresses [X], but what we actually needed was [Y]"** = "You did something, but it's not what we needed at all"

- **"Let's talk through the original request so we're aligned on the business goal behind this project"** = "I need to explain the real purpose of this project because you clearly didn't get it"

More Direct: "We need to recalibrate on this project. The work you've done doesn't align with what we need to accomplish. I think we got our wires crossed on the core objective. Let me clarify: we need [specific outcome] because [business reason]. What you've created focuses on [what they did instead], which isn't going to achieve that goal."

What you're communicating: "This is off track and we need to reset. What you made doesn't do what we need it to do. There was confusion about the main goal. Here's what we're actually trying to accomplish and why. What you did is something totally different and won't work for what we need."

Breaking it down:

- **"We need to recalibrate on this project"** = "We need to stop and redirect because this is going the wrong way"
- **"The work you've done doesn't align with what we need to accomplish"** = "What you made doesn't match what we're trying to do"
- **"We got our wires crossed on the core objective"** = "There was confusion about the main point of this whole project"
- **"Let me clarify: we need [specific outcome] because [business reason]"** = "Let me tell you clearly what we're actually trying to do and why it matters"
- **"What you've created focuses on [what they did instead], which isn't going to achieve that goal"** = "You made something that focuses on the wrong thing, and it won't help us reach our actual goal"

Firm: "Unfortunately, this misses the mark and doesn't address what we're trying to accomplish. Before you spend more time on this, I need to ensure you understand what we're actually trying to accomplish and why. Let's back up and review the project scope and objectives, because the current direction isn't going to get us the results we need."

What you're communicating: "This is wrong and doesn't solve the actual problem. Before you waste more time, I need to make sure you understand what we're really trying to do and why it matters. Let's go back to the beginning and review what this project is supposed to be, because what you're doing now won't work."

Breaking it down:

- **"Unfortunately, this misses the mark"** = "This is not what we needed—you got it wrong"
- **"Doesn't address what we're trying to accomplish"** = "This doesn't solve the actual problem we're trying to fix"
- **"Before you spend more time on this, I need to ensure you understand"** = "Stop working on this right now until I make sure you get what we're actually doing"
- **"What we're actually trying to accomplish and why"** = "The real goal and the reason behind it, which you clearly don't understand"
- **"Let's back up and review the project scope and objectives"** = "Let's start over from the beginning and go through what this project is supposed to be"
- **"The current direction isn't going to get us the results we need"** = "What you're doing now is wrong and won't give us what we need"

Why This Works: You're acknowledging their effort without validating the quality. The phrase "miscommunication" or "misalignment" removes the blame element while still making it clear that the work doesn't work. You're redirecting to the "why" behind the project, which helps them understand they missed the strategic point, not just made some formatting errors.

Scenario 3: Faster to Redo Than Fix

Situation: An employee delivered work that's so far off base that you've realized it would actually take less time to do it yourself from scratch than to explain everything that's wrong and guide them through fixing it. The errors aren't just surface-level—they demonstrate a lack of understanding of basic concepts required for the job.

What You're Thinking: "I could literally do this myself in 30 minutes, and it would take me three hours to explain to you what's wrong with this and supervise the fixes. This is the opposite of delegation efficiency. Why are you in this role?"

What You Should Say:

Diplomatic: "I'm seeing some fundamental gaps in how this was approached. Rather than spending time on extensive revisions, I think it would be more valuable for you to watch how I work through this type of task. I'm going to rebuild this one as a model, and then you'll take the lead on the next one with the benefit of having seen the complete process."

What you're communicating: "You don't understand the basics of how to do this. Instead of trying to fix all your mistakes (which would take forever), I'm just going to do it myself while you watch. Then maybe you'll understand how it's supposed to be done, and you can try again next time."

Breaking it down:

- **"I'm seeing some fundamental gaps in how this was approached"** = "You don't understand the basic concepts needed to do this job"
- **"Rather than spending time on extensive revisions"** = "Rather than wasting time trying to fix all the problems in your work"
- **"I think it would be more valuable for you to watch how I work through this"** = "You need to see how to actually do this correctly because you clearly don't know"

- **"I'm going to rebuild this one as a model"** = "I'm going to do it myself from scratch, and you're going to watch"
- **"You'll take the lead on the next one with the benefit of having seen the complete process"** = "After watching me do it right, you can try again and hopefully not mess it up this time"

More Direct: "This work shows me we need to reset on the foundational skills for this type of task. The issues here aren't quick fixes—they indicate we need to take a step back and ensure you have a solid grasp of [specific skill/concept]. I'm going to handle this particular deliverable, and then we're going to set up training time so you have what you need to successfully complete these assignments going forward."

What you're communicating: "This work proves you don't have the basic skills you need for this job. The problems aren't small things I can help you fix—they show you don't understand the fundamentals. I'm taking over this project, and then we need to get you trained on the basics because you clearly don't have them."

Breaking it down:

- **"This work shows me we need to reset on the foundational skills for this type of task"** = "Your work proves you don't have the basic skills required"
- **"The issues here aren't quick fixes"** = "The problems are too big and too many to just correct"
- **"They indicate we need to take a step back and ensure you have a solid grasp"** = "They show you don't understand the fundamentals, so we need to go back to basics"
- **"I'm going to handle this particular deliverable"** = "I'm taking this away from you and doing it myself"
- **"We're going to set up training time"** = "You need to learn the basic skills you should already have"
- **"So you have what you need to successfully complete these assignments going forward"** = "So you can actually do your job properly in the future"

Firm: "I need to be direct: this work demonstrates a gap in core competencies that are essential for your role. The errors here aren't about inexperience with our systems or minor oversights—they reflect a misunderstanding of fundamental concepts. I'm going to take this one over, and then you and I need to have a broader conversation about the skills and knowledge you need to develop to meet the requirements of this position."

What you're communicating: "Let me be blunt: this work shows you don't have the basic skills your job requires. These aren't small mistakes or things you'll learn with time—these are fundamental problems that show you don't understand core concepts. I'm doing this work myself, and then we need to have a serious talk about whether you have what it takes to do this job and what needs to change."

Breaking it down:

- **"I need to be direct"** = "I'm going to be honest with you in a way that might be uncomfortable"
- **"This work demonstrates a gap in core competencies that are essential for your role"** = "This proves you're missing basic skills that your job absolutely requires"
- **"The errors here aren't about inexperience with our systems or minor oversights"** = "These aren't small mistakes or things you'd know with more time here"
- **"They reflect a misunderstanding of fundamental concepts"** = "They show you don't understand the basic principles of this work"
- **"I'm going to take this one over"** = "I'm doing this myself because you can't"
- **"We need to have a broader conversation about the skills and knowledge you need to develop"** = "We need to have a serious discussion about what you're lacking and whether you can improve enough to keep this job"
- **"To meet the requirements of this position"** = "To actually be able to do what you were hired to do"

Why This Works: You're being honest that the work isn't fixable without saying "you're incompetent." The framing of "gaps in foundational skills" or "core competencies" makes it clear this is serious without being personally attacking. Taking over the work yourself is positioned as a teaching opportunity, not as "you're so hopeless I have to do it myself." The firmest version acknowledges this is a capability issue that needs to be addressed, which documents the concern while giving them a chance to improve.

Scenario 4: The "Did You Even Read the Instructions?" Situation

Situation: An employee completed a task in a way that clearly indicates they didn't read the instructions, follow the process, or pay attention to the requirements you outlined. Maybe they used the wrong template, ignored specified parameters, or did their own thing entirely. It's not a judgment call difference—they objectively didn't do what was asked.

What You're Thinking: "Did you even glance at the instructions? This isn't a matter of interpretation—you literally didn't do what I asked you to do. Do you just not read emails? Do you think the requirements are optional? Should I start communicating with you exclusively in crayon?"

What You Should Say:

Diplomatic: "I want to make sure we're on the same page about the requirements for this task. When I compare what you've submitted to the specifications I outlined, I'm seeing some significant differences. Can you walk me through your process? I want to understand if the instructions were unclear or if there were factors I'm not aware of."

What you're communicating: "What you did doesn't match what I asked you to do at all. I want to understand what happened—did you not understand the instructions, or did you just ignore them? I'm giving you a chance to explain before I assume you just didn't bother to read what I sent."

Breaking it down:

- **"I want to make sure we're on the same page about the requirements"** = "I need to check if you understood what I asked you to do, because it doesn't look like you did"
- **"When I compare what you've submitted to the specifications I outlined, I'm seeing some significant differences"** = "What you turned in is completely different from what I asked for"
- **"Can you walk me through your process?"** = "Explain to me how you ended up doing this instead of what I asked"
- **"I want to understand if the instructions were unclear or if there were factors I'm not aware of"** = "I'm checking if maybe I wasn't clear enough, or if you have some excuse for why you didn't follow the directions"

More Direct: "This doesn't align with the instructions provided. The task specifically called for [X, Y, Z], and what I'm seeing is [A, B, C]. Before we go further, I need to understand: did you review the full requirements document I sent? Because this appears to have been completed without reference to those specifications."

What you're communicating: "This is not what I asked for. I specifically told you to do [X, Y, Z], and you did [A, B, C] instead. I need to know: Did you actually read the instructions I gave you? Because it really looks like you didn't even look at them."

Breaking it down:

- **"This doesn't align with the instructions provided"** = "This is not what I told you to do"
- **"The task specifically called for [X, Y, Z], and what I'm seeing is [A, B, C]"** = "I clearly asked for these specific things, and you did completely different things instead"
- **"Before we go further, I need to understand: did you review the full requirements document I sent?"** = "Did you actually read what I sent you, or did you just skip it?"

- **"This appears to have been completed without reference to those specifications"** = "It looks like you didn't look at the instructions at all"

Firm: "We have a problem. The work you've submitted doesn't follow the requirements I provided. This isn't a stylistic difference—the fundamental parameters were not followed. Going forward, I need you to carefully review all instructions before beginning work and confirm with me if anything is unclear. For this task, you'll need to start over using the correct specifications. This is the time we can't afford to lose on preventable errors."

What you're communicating: "This is a serious issue. You didn't do what I told you to do. This isn't about doing it differently than I would—you ignored the basic requirements. From now on, you need to actually read the instructions before you start, and ask me if you don't understand something. You need to redo this completely and do it right this time. We're wasting time because you didn't pay attention to what you were supposed to do."

Breaking it down:

- **"We have a problem"** = "This is serious and I'm not happy about it"
- **"The work you've submitted doesn't follow the requirements I provided"** = "You didn't do what I told you to do"
- **"This isn't a stylistic difference—the fundamental parameters were not followed"** = "This isn't about personal preference—you ignored the basic requirements"
- **"Going forward, I need you to carefully review all instructions before beginning work"** = "From now on, you need to actually read what I send you before you start working"
- **"Confirm with me if anything is unclear"** = "Ask me questions if you don't understand, instead of just guessing or ignoring the instructions"

- **"You'll need to start over using the correct specifications"** = "You have to do this again from scratch, and this time follow the actual requirements"
- **"This is time we can't afford to lose on preventable errors"** = "You're wasting our time with mistakes that shouldn't have happened if you'd just paid attention"

Why This Works: The diplomatic version opens the door to legitimate reasons (maybe the instructions were unclear, maybe they had technical issues accessing the requirements). The direct version puts the question out there without being accusatory. The firm version makes it clear that not following instructions is a serious issue without saying "you're careless" or "you don't pay attention." In all versions, you're focusing on the objective gap between requirements and deliverables.

Scenario 5: Careless Errors Everywhere

Situation: The work is full of preventable mistakes—typos, wrong numbers, dates that don't match, names misspelled, and calculations that are off. These aren't skill gaps; they're just sloppiness. It's clear they didn't proofread, double-check, or put in the minimum quality control effort.

What You're Thinking: "Did you even glance at this before hitting send? How do you submit work with someone's name spelled wrong in the subject line? With numbers that any reasonable person would double-check? This is just lazy. Do you not care? Do you think someone else's job is to catch your mistakes?"

What You Should Say:

Diplomatic: "I'm noticing a number of errors in this work that should have been caught in review—incorrect dates, calculation mistakes, and several typos. Accuracy and attention to detail are critical for this type of deliverable. Before submitting work going forward, please build in time to thoroughly proofread and verify all data. These types of errors undermine the quality of the work and create additional correction time for everyone."

What you're communicating: "This work is full of careless mistakes that you should have caught before sending it to me—wrong dates, bad math, and typos everywhere. Being accurate and careful matters for this kind of work. From now on, you need to actually check your work before you turn it in. These sloppy errors make the work look bad and mean someone else has to spend time fixing your mistakes."

Breaking it down:

- **"I'm noticing a number of errors in this work that should have been caught in review"** = "There are a lot of mistakes that you should have found yourself before sending this to me"
- **"Incorrect dates, calculation mistakes, and several typos"** = "Wrong dates, bad math, and spelling errors"
- **"Accuracy and attention to detail are critical for this type of deliverable"** = "You need to be careful and accurate with this kind of work—it matters"
- **"Please build in time to thoroughly proofread and verify all data"** = "Actually check your work before you submit it"
- **"These types of errors undermine the quality of the work"** = "These sloppy mistakes make the work look bad"
- **"Create additional correction time for everyone"** = "Someone else has to waste time fixing your careless errors"

More Direct: "This work has too many preventable errors to be acceptable. I'm seeing [specific examples]. These are quality control issues that need to be caught before work is submitted, not after. I need you to implement a review process—whatever that looks like for you—because the error rate here isn't sustainable."

What you're communicating: "There are way too many careless mistakes in this for me to accept it. Look at [specific examples]. These are things you should catch yourself before you turn work in, not things I should have to point out. You need to figure out a way to check your own work—I don't care how you do it—because you're making too many mistakes for this to continue."

Breaking it down:

- **"This work has too many preventable errors to be acceptable"** = "There are so many careless mistakes that I can't accept this work"
- **"I'm seeing [specific examples]"** = "Here are the actual mistakes you made"
- **"These are quality control issues that need to be caught before work is submitted, not after"** = "You should be catching these yourself before sending it to me, not making me find them"
- **"I need you to implement a review process—whatever that looks like for you"** = "Figure out a way to check your own work—I don't care what method you use"
- **"The error rate here isn't sustainable"** = "You're making too many mistakes for this to keep happening"

Firm: "We need to address the accuracy issues in your work. This submission contains [X number] of errors that should have been caught through basic review. This pattern of careless mistakes is impacting our team's efficiency and credibility. Going forward, I expect you to thoroughly review all work before submission. If you're unclear about our quality standards, we need to discuss that now, because this level of accuracy is a fundamental requirement of your role."

What you're communicating: "We have a serious problem with how sloppy your work is. This has [X number] of mistakes that you should have caught by just checking it once. You keep making careless errors, and it's making our whole team look bad and slowing us down. From now on, you better carefully check your work before you give it to me. If you don't understand what 'good enough' looks like, we need to talk about that right now, because being accurate is a basic part of your job that you have to do."

Breaking it down:

- **"We need to address the accuracy issues in your work"** = "Your sloppy, careless work is a problem we have to fix"

- **"This submission contains [X number] of errors that should have been caught through basic review"** = "There are [X] mistakes in this that you would have found if you'd just looked it over once"
- **"This pattern of careless mistakes is impacting our team's efficiency and credibility"** = "You keep making sloppy errors, and it's making our team look bad and wasting everyone's time"
- **"Going forward, I expect you to thoroughly review all work before submission"** = "From now on, you need to carefully check everything before you turn it in"
- **"If you're unclear about our quality standards, we need to discuss that now"** = "If you don't know what acceptable work looks like, tell me now so we can talk about it"
- **"This level of accuracy is a fundamental requirement of your role"** = "Being accurate and careful is a basic part of your job—not optional"

Why This Works: You're calling out the specific problem (errors that should have been caught) without saying "you're sloppy" or "you don't care." The phrase "attention to detail" is HR-speak for "you're making stupid mistakes," but it's professional enough to use. You're making it clear this is a performance issue without making it personal, and you're setting an explicit expectation for their own quality control process.

Scenario 6: They Don't Grasp Job Basics

Situation: The work consistently demonstrates that the employee doesn't understand fundamental concepts of their role. This isn't new hire confusion—they've been here long enough that they should have these basics down. But every project reveals that they still don't get the core principles that are essential for their job.

What You're Thinking: "How are you still employed here? This is literally what you were hired to do, and you don't understand the basic concepts. A new grad would know this. Did you lie on your resume? Should I be concerned about what else you don't know?"

What You Should Say:

Diplomatic: "I'm seeing a pattern in the work you're submitting that suggests we need to revisit some foundational concepts for this role. The approaches you're taking indicate there may be some knowledge gaps in [specific area]. Let's set up some time for me to walk you through the core principles of [X], because having a solid grasp of these fundamentals is essential for the work we need you to do."

What you're communicating: "Your work keeps showing that you don't understand the basics of this job. The way you're doing things proves you're missing important knowledge about [specific area]. I need to teach you the fundamental concepts of [X] because you clearly don't know them, and you can't do this job without understanding these basics."

Breaking it down:

- **"I'm seeing a pattern in the work you're submitting"** = "This keeps happening—it's not just one mistake"
- **"That suggests we need to revisit some foundational concepts for this role"** = "That shows you don't understand the basic things you should know for this job"
- **"The approaches you're taking indicate there may be some knowledge gaps"** = "The way you're doing things proves you don't know important things about this work"
- **"Let's set up some time for me to walk you through the core principles"** = "I need to teach you the fundamental concepts because you don't know them"
- **"Having a solid grasp of these fundamentals is essential for the work we need you to do"** = "You have to understand these basics to be able to do your job"

More Direct: "I need to be honest with you: the work you're producing shows a lack of understanding of core concepts that are essential for your position. This isn't about mastering advanced techniques—these are the fundamentals of [job function]. We need to address this gap directly. I'm going to arrange training on [specific areas], and I need you to prioritize developing these skills because they're non-negotiable requirements for this role."

What you're communicating: "Let me be straight with you: your work proves you don't understand basic concepts that your job requires. I'm not talking about expert-level stuff—I'm talking about the fundamental basics of [job function]. This is a real problem we have to fix. I'm going to get you training on [specific areas], and you need to make learning these skills your top priority because you absolutely must have them to do this job."

Breaking it down:

- **"I need to be honest with you"** = "I'm going to tell you something directly that might be uncomfortable"
- **"The work you're producing shows a lack of understanding of core concepts"** = "Your work proves you don't understand the basic ideas"
- **"That is essential for your position"** = "That's core to your position"
- **"This isn't about mastering advanced techniques—these are the fundamentals"** = "I'm not talking about complicated expert stuff—I'm talking about the basics"
- **"We need to address this gap directly"** = "We have to fix this problem head-on"
- **"I'm going to arrange training on [specific areas]"** = "I'm going to get you training because you need to learn this"
- **"I need you to prioritize developing these skills"** = "You need to make learning this your most important task"
- **"They're non-negotiable requirements for this role"** = "You must have these skills—there's no way around it"

Firm: "We have a serious skills gap that needs to be addressed. Your work consistently shows that you're missing fundamental knowledge in areas that are central to your job responsibilities. This is affecting not just the quality of your deliverables but also our team's capacity and output. I need to see significant improvement in your grasp of [specific concepts/skills] within [timeframe]. I'm going to provide resources and training, but I need you to understand this is a critical performance issue that must be resolved."

What you're communicating: "This is a major problem. Your work keeps proving that you don't have basic knowledge about things that are at the core of what you're supposed to do. This isn't just about your work being bad—it's hurting what our whole team can accomplish. You need to get much better at [specific concepts/skills] by [timeframe], or else. I'm going to give you resources and training, but you need to understand this is a serious performance problem that has to be fixed."

Breaking it down:

- **"We have a serious skills gap that needs to be addressed"** = "You're missing important skills, and this is a big problem"
- **"Your work consistently shows that you're missing fundamental knowledge"** = "Your work keeps proving you don't have basic knowledge"
- **"In areas that are central to your job responsibilities"** = "About things that are at the core of what your job is"
- **"This is affecting not just the quality of your deliverables but also our team's capacity and output"** = "This isn't just about your bad work—it's hurting what our whole team can get done"
- **"I need to see significant improvement in your grasp of [specific concepts/skills] within [timeframe]"** = "You need to get a lot better at [specific concepts/skills] by [timeframe]"
- **"I'm going to provide resources and training"** = "I'll give you materials and training to help you"
- **"I need you to understand this is a critical performance issue that must be resolved"** = "You need to know this is a serious problem with your job performance that has to be fixed"

Why This Works: You're clearly identifying this as a capability problem without saying "you're not qualified for this job" or "you don't know what you're doing." The focus on "foundational concepts" and "core principles" makes it clear this is basic stuff they should know, not advanced expertise. The firm version explicitly calls it a performance issue, which is important for documentation purposes if this doesn't improve, while still giving them a path forward.

HR-APPROVED PHRASE COLLECTION

Instead of "This is wrong/terrible/unacceptable"

A. "This doesn't meet our quality standards."
B. "This isn't at the level we need for [client review / executive presentation / external submission]."
C. "We need to significantly revise this before it's ready."
D. "This requires substantial rework."
E. "The current version isn't usable for our purposes."
F. "This deliverable doesn't align with our requirements."
G. "We have some significant gaps between what was submitted and what we need."
H. "This isn't going to work for our business objectives."
I. "The quality here isn't consistent with expectations for this role."
J. "This misses the mark on several critical elements."

Instead of "You didn't think this through"

A. "I'm not seeing evidence that the approach was fully thought through."
B. "This could benefit from more strategic thinking about [X]."
C. "The logic flow here isn't clear to me."
D. "I'd like to understand the reasoning behind this approach."
E. "This seems to jump to conclusions without showing the analysis."

F. "We're missing some critical thinking steps between the problem and the solution."
G. "The approach here feels rushed—like we skipped some important planning stages."
H. "This would be stronger with more consideration of [X, Y, Z factors]."
I. "I'm not seeing the level of analysis we need for this type of decision."

Instead of "You clearly don't understand this"

A. "I think we have some misalignment on the core concepts here."
B. "This suggests we need to revisit the fundamentals of [X]."
C. "There seems to be a gap in understanding about how this process works."
D. "I'm seeing some confusion about the key principles of [X]."
E. "Let's make sure we're aligned on what [X concept] means in practice."
F. "This approach tells me we need to spend more time on the foundational knowledge."
G. "I want to ensure you have a solid grasp of the underlying concepts before we move forward."
H. "It looks like there may be some knowledge gaps we need to address."
I. "This indicates we need to build stronger foundational skills in [area]."

Instead of "A child could have done better"

A. "This doesn't reflect the level of capability expected for this role."
B. "We need work that demonstrates more advanced [analytical/technical/strategic] skills."

C. "This is more basic than what we need from someone at your level."
D. "I'm looking for more sophisticated thinking on this."
E. "This approach is too elementary for the complexity of the task."
F. "We need work that shows stronger professional judgment."
G. "This doesn't demonstrate the level of expertise required for your position."
H. "I'd expect to see more advanced capabilities at this stage."

Instead of "Did you even try?"

A. "This seems incomplete. Can you walk me through what you've completed so far?"
B. "I'm not seeing the level of effort that this project requires."
C. "This feels like a first draft rather than a final submission."
D. "I'd like to understand the amount of time you invested in this."
E. "This appears rushed. What was your timeline for completing this work?"
F. "The thoroughness here doesn't match the scope of the assignment."
G. "I need to see more depth in your work on this."

Instead of "You're making stupid mistakes"

A. "I'm seeing a pattern of preventable errors that need to be addressed."
B. "The accuracy rate here isn't meeting our standards."
C. "We need to strengthen attention to detail in your work."
D. "These types of quality control issues are becoming a concern."
E. "I need you to implement a more thorough review process before submission."
F. "The error rate is too high for this type of work."

G. "Accuracy is critical here, and we're not seeing that consistently."
H. "These mistakes are avoidable with proper quality control."
I. "We need to see more careful work from you."
J. "The proofreading and verification step seems to be getting missed."

Instead of "This makes no sense"

A. "I'm having difficulty following the logic here."
B. "The organization of this needs work—I'm not able to extract the key points."
C. "This would benefit from a clearer structure."
D. "I'm not able to follow your line of reasoning."
E. "The flow of information here is confusing."
F. "This needs to be reorganized for clarity."
G. "I'm getting lost in the presentation of this information."
H. "The key messages are getting buried—we need to bring them forward."
I. "This needs a clearer narrative structure."

Instead of "You missed the entire point"

A. "I think we got our wires crossed on the objective here."
B. "This addresses [X], but what we actually needed was [Y]."
C. "There's a disconnect between this deliverable and the business goal."
D. "This doesn't align with the core objective we discussed."
E. "We need to recalibrate on what this project is meant to accomplish."
F. "The focus here isn't quite right for what we're trying to achieve."
G. "This is solving for a different problem than the one we have."
H. "We've veered off course from the original goal."
I. "The strategic purpose is getting lost here."

Instead of "Start over"

A. "We need to take a different approach to this."
B. "Let's rebuild this from a new foundation."
C. "I think we need to go back to the drawing board on this one."
D. "This needs to be reworked from the ground up."
E. "We should restart this with a clearer framework."
F. "Let's reset and begin with a different strategy."
G. "This requires a fresh start with better alignment on objectives."

Instead of "You don't have the skills for this"

A. "This task requires capabilities we need to develop."
B. "There's a skills gap here that we need to address."
C. "You'll need additional training in [area] to successfully complete this type of work."
D. "This is revealing some developmental needs in [X]."
E. "We need to build your proficiency in [skill] before you can take on these tasks independently."
F. "This level of work requires expertise that needs to be strengthened."
G. "There are core competencies for this role that need development."

When you need to be more direct about capability concerns

A. "I'm not seeing the level of performance expected for this role."
B. "There's a significant gap between the work you're producing and the standards for this position."
C. "This is a fundamental performance issue we need to address."
D. "The quality of work is below what's required for your job level."
E. "We have concerns about whether you have the core capabilities this role demands."

F. "This pattern of work is raising questions about fit for this position."
G. "The skill level demonstrated here isn't meeting the requirements of the role."

Phrases for "The instructions were clear and you ignored them"

A. "This doesn't align with the specifications provided."
B. "I'm not seeing the requirements reflected in this work."
C. "This appears to have been completed without reference to the guidelines."
D. "The parameters we discussed aren't present in this deliverable."
E. "This doesn't follow the process we outlined."
F. "The format/approach here doesn't match what was requested."
G. "Before we continue, I need to ensure the instructions were clear—because this work doesn't reflect them."

Phrases for "This is embarrassingly bad"

A. "This isn't at a level we can present to [stakeholders/clients/executives]."
B. "The quality here would damage our credibility."
C. "This doesn't reflect professional standards."
D. "We can't move forward with work at this level."
E. "This would not make a good impression on our audience."
F. "The standard here is below what our [clients/leadership/partners] would expect."
G. "This needs to be at a level that represents our team well."

Phrases for showing them what good looks like

A. "Let me show you an example of what meets our standards."

B. "Here's what a strong version of this looks like."
C. "I'm going to walk you through what good performance on this task entails."
D. "Let's review a model that demonstrates the quality we're looking for."
E. "I want to calibrate your expectations by showing you what excellent work on this looks like."
F. "Here's the benchmark for this type of deliverable."

Quick Reference Box

Ten Essential Phrases for Substandard Work

1. "This doesn't meet our quality standards and needs significant revision."

2. "There's a gap between this deliverable and what we need—let's talk about how to close it."

3. "I'm seeing patterns of preventable errors that we need to address."

4. "This indicates some foundational knowledge gaps we should work on."

5. "The quality here isn't consistent with expectations for this role."

6. "We got our wires crossed on the objective—let me clarify what we're actually trying to accomplish."

7. "Before you spend more time on this, let me show you what good looks like."

8. "This isn't at the level we can present to [stakeholders], so we need substantial rework."

9. "The approach here doesn't align with the requirements I outlined—let's make sure we're on the same page."
10. "I need to be direct: this is a performance issue we have to address, because the work isn't meeting the standards required for your position."

TWO
ADDRESSING SLOW WORKERS & LOW PRODUCTIVITY

"Let's Discuss Your Efficiency" (Translation: Why Does This Take You So Long?)

Real Talk

There's nothing quite like watching someone take an entire day to complete a task that should take an hour. You've seen other team members knock out the same assignment over lunch. You've watched new hires figure it out faster. And yet here's this employee, still plugging away, asking for extensions, acting like they're climbing Everest when everyone else is taking the stairs.

Maybe they're genuinely working the whole time—just incredibly slowly. Maybe they're getting lost in unnecessary details. Maybe they lack basic efficiency instincts that would tell them "this approach is taking way too long." Or maybe they're just not working as much as they claim to be. Either way, the end result is the same: tasks that should take hours are taking days, projects are falling behind, and you're stuck either picking up the slack or constantly explaining to your own boss why deadlines are slipping.

You obviously can't say "you're painfully slow," or "why does this take you forever?" or "everyone else finished this in two hours—what's your excuse?" But you also can't let someone operate at half speed indefinitely when it's affecting team productivity and your ability to deliver. This chapter gives you the language to address speed and efficiency issues without sounding like a taskmaster or creating a hostile work environment claim.

Five Principles for the Productivity Conversation

- **Focus on output and timelines, not perceived effort.** Don't question how hard they're working—focus on what's getting delivered and when.

- **Use objective benchmarks when possible.** "This typically takes 2-3 hours" is stronger than "I feel like you're slow."

- **Distinguish between learning curves and chronic slowness.** New tasks take longer—that's normal. But if they're still slow after doing something ten times, that's a different conversation.

- **Address the impact, not just the behavior.** Explain how the slow pace affects projects, team capacity, and business outcomes.

- **Offer process help before assuming incompetence.** Sometimes people are slow because they don't know more efficient methods. Give them tools before concluding they just can't pick up the pace.

Let's Get Real Scenarios

Scenario 1: The Same Task Takes Them 4x Longer Than Everyone Else

Situation: You've noticed a consistent pattern: tasks that take most people 1-2 hours are taking this employee 6-8 hours. It's not a one-time thing—it happens with every assignment. They're not producing higher-quality work to justify the extra time; they're just slow. And it's starting to impact what you can assign them and how you plan project timelines.

What You're Thinking: "How is it possible that this takes you an entire day? I've literally watched three other people do this same task in under two hours. Are you taking a nap in the middle? Are you counting grains of sand? What is happening during all that time?"

What You Should Say:

Diplomatic: "I want to talk about timelines for [task type]. I'm noticing these assignments are taking significantly longer than our typical benchmark. Most team members complete this in about [X hours], and I'm seeing it's taking you closer to [Y hours]. Can you walk me through your process? I want to understand if there are obstacles I'm not aware of, or if there are efficiency strategies we can implement."

What you're communicating: "You're taking way too long to do this work. Other people finish this task much faster than you do. Tell me what you're doing during all that time. Is something blocking you, or do you just not know how to work efficiently? Either way, we need to figure out how to speed you up."

Breaking it down:

- **"I want to talk about timelines"** = "We need to discuss how slow you are"

- **"These assignments are taking significantly longer than our typical benchmark"** = "You're taking way longer than normal to finish these"
- **"Most team members complete this in about [X hours], and I'm seeing it's taking you closer to [Y hours]"** = "Everyone else finishes this fast, but you're taking forever"
- **"Can you walk me through your process?"** = "Explain to me what you're doing that takes so long"
- **"I want to understand if there are obstacles I'm not aware of"** = "Tell me if something's blocking you, or admit you just work slowly"
- **"Or if there are efficiency strategies we can implement"** = "Or if we need to teach you how to work faster"

More Direct: "We need to address the time it's taking you to complete [task type]. The current pace isn't sustainable for our team's workload. This task has a standard completion time of [X hours], and you're consistently exceeding that by a significant margin. I need to understand what's driving the timeline difference so we can get you working at the pace this role requires."

What you're communicating: "You're too slow, and we need to fix this problem. How long you're taking doesn't work for what our team needs to get done. This task should take [X hours], and you're taking way longer every single time. I need to know why you're so slow so we can figure out how to get you working at normal speed for this job."

Breaking it down:

- **"We need to address the time it's taking you"** = "Your slowness is a problem we have to fix"
- **"The current pace isn't sustainable for our team's workload"** = "You working this slowly doesn't work for what we need to accomplish"
- **"This task has a standard completion time of [X hours]"** = "There's a normal amount of time this should take"

- **"You're consistently exceeding that by a significant margin"** = "You're taking way longer than you should, and it keeps happening"
- **"I need to understand what's driving the timeline difference"** = "I need to know why you're so much slower than everyone else"
- **"So we can get you working at the pace this role requires"** = "So we can figure out how to speed you up to where you need to be"

Firm: "Your completion times are significantly impacting our team's capacity. Tasks that should take [X timeframe] are consistently taking you [Y timeframe]. This isn't about working faster at the expense of quality—this is about working at the standard pace for this role. I need to see your turnaround times come down to match team benchmarks within [timeframe]. Let's identify what needs to change to make that happen, so that we address this performance issue."

What you're communicating: "Let me be blunt about this problem: you're way too slow and it's hurting what our whole team can get done. Work that should take [X time] keeps taking you [Y time]. I'm not asking you to rush and do sloppy work—I'm asking you to work at normal speed for this job. You need to get a lot faster within [timeframe]. Let's figure out what has to change for you to speed up."

Breaking it down:

- **"Your completion times are significantly impacting our team's capacity"** = "How slow you are is hurting what our team can accomplish"
- **"Tasks that should take [X timeframe] are consistently taking you [Y timeframe]"** = "Work that should take [X time] keeps taking you way longer—[Y time]"
- **"This isn't about working faster at the expense of quality"** = "I'm not asking you to rush and do bad work"
- **"This is about working at the standard pace for this role"** = "This is about working at normal speed for this job"

- **"I need to see your turnaround times come down to match team benchmarks within [timeframe]"** = "You need to get much faster by [timeframe] to be within a similar range of how fast everyone else works"
- **"Let's identify what needs to change to make that happen, so that we address performance issue"** = "Let's figure out what has to change for you to speed up and fix this problem because it is clearly a performance issue"

Why This Works: You're using objective time comparisons rather than subjective judgments about effort. By referencing team benchmarks or standard completion times, you're making it about data, not perception. The diplomatic version opens the door to legitimate obstacles, the direct version makes expectations clear, and the firm version establishes this as a performance issue with a timeline for improvement.

Scenario 2: They Need Constant Hand-Holding on Routine Work

Situation: This employee needs excessive guidance and check-ins for tasks they've done multiple times before. They ask questions that they should know the answers to by now. They seek approval at every step instead of just doing the work. The hand-holding is eating up your time and slowing down projects because they can't seem to work independently, even on routine assignments.

What You're Thinking: "You've done this exact task six times already. Why are you asking me to walk you through it again? Why do you need me to approve every single step? Other people figured this out on their second try. Do you need a written instruction manual for tying your shoes, too?"

What You Should Say:

Diplomatic: "I want to help you build more independence with [task type]. You've completed this several times now, and I think you're ready to work through it without as much guidance. I'm going to step back on check-ins for this assignment so you can develop confidence working through it on your own. If you hit a genuine roadblock, absolutely reach out—but try working through the routine steps independently first."

What you're communicating: "You need to stop asking me for help on every little thing with this task. You've done this enough times that you should be able to do it yourself now. I'm not going to keep checking in with you and holding your hand through it—you need to learn to do this on your own. If you get really stuck, fine, ask me—but try to figure it out yourself first instead of running to me constantly."

Breaking it down:

- **"I want to help you build more independence"** = "You need to stop relying on me so much"
- **"You've completed this several times now"** = "You've done this enough times already"
- **"I think you're ready to work through it without as much guidance"** = "You should be able to do this without me holding your hand"
- **"I'm going to step back on check-ins for this assignment"** = "I'm not going to keep checking on you and helping you through every step"
- **"So you can develop confidence working through it on your own"** = "So you can learn to do this yourself"
- **"If you hit a genuine roadblock, absolutely reach out"** = "If you really get stuck, you can ask me"
- **"But try working through the routine steps independently first"** = "But try to figure it out on your own first instead of immediately asking for help"

More Direct: "We need to shift how you approach [task type]. At this point, you've completed this [X times], and you should be able to execute it independently without step-by-step guidance. The level of oversight you're requiring isn't appropriate for someone at your experience level with this task. I need you to work through this on your own and only escalate when you encounter something truly unfamiliar or problematic."

What you're communicating: "You need to change how you do this task. By now, you've done this [X times], so you should be able to do it by yourself without me walking you through each step. How much you need me to supervise you doesn't make sense for someone who's done this as many times as you have. You need to do this yourself and only come to me if you run into something you genuinely don't know or a real problem."

Breaking it down:

- **"We need to shift how you approach this"** = "You need to change how you handle this task"
- **"At this point, you've completed this [X times]"** = "You've done this [X times] already—that's enough"
- **"You should be able to execute it independently without step-by-step guidance"** = "You should be able to do it by yourself without me guiding you through every step"
- **"The level of oversight you're requiring isn't appropriate"** = "How much supervision you need doesn't make sense"
- **"For someone at your experience level with this task"** = "For someone who's done this as many times as you have"
- **"I need you to work through this on your own"** = "You need to do this by yourself"
- **"And only escalate when you encounter something truly unfamiliar or problematic"** = "And only ask me when you hit something you really don't know or a real problem"

Firm: "I need to address the amount of guidance you're requiring for work that's become routine. You've completed [task] multiple times, yet you're still asking for the same level of direction as someone doing it for the first time. This is impacting both your efficiency and mine. Going forward, I expect you to execute [task type] independently. You have the resources and experience you need. The constant check-ins need to stop—this should be something you can handle on your own at this point."

What you're communicating: "We need to talk about how much you keep asking me for help on work you should know how to do. You've done [task] many times, but you're still acting like you're doing it for the first time and need me to walk you through everything. This is making you slow and wasting my time, too. From now on, I expect you to do [task type] by yourself. You know how to do this, and you have what you need. Stop constantly checking in with me—you should be able to handle this on your own by now."

Breaking it down:

- **"I need to address the amount of guidance you're requiring"** = "We need to talk about how much you keep asking me for help"
- **"For work that's become routine"** = "On work you should know how to do by now"
- **"Yet you're still asking for the same level of direction as someone doing it for the first time"** = "But you're still acting like you're brand new to this and need me to guide you through everything"
- **"This is impacting both your efficiency and mine"** = "This is making you slow, and it's wasting my time too"
- **"Going forward, I expect you to execute [task type] independently"** = "From now on, you need to do this yourself"
- **"You have the resources and experience you need"** = "You already know how to do this and have what you need"
- **"The constant check-ins need to stop"** = "Stop coming to me all the time"
- **"This should be something you can handle on your own at this point"** = "You should be able to do this by yourself now"

Why This Works: You're highlighting the disconnect between their experience level and the amount of support they're seeking. By framing it as building independence rather than "stop bothering me," you're making it about professional development. The firm version makes it clear that the hand-holding has to end and sets the expectation for independent work going forward.

Scenario 3: Everything Becomes an Epic Undertaking

Situation: This employee approaches every task like it's a major research project. They overcomplicate simple assignments, get lost in unnecessary details, and spend time on things that don't matter. What should be a straightforward 30-minute task turns into a multi-hour production because they can't distinguish between what's essential and what's extra.

What You're Thinking: "Why are you making this so complicated? This is not that deep. You don't need to analyze seventeen variables for a task that requires three. You're not writing a dissertation—just answer the question and move on. Do you not understand what 'quick turnaround' means?"

What You Should Say:

Diplomatic: "I want to help you calibrate your approach for different types of assignments. I'm noticing that tasks designed to be quick and straightforward are becoming more involved than they need to be. For something like [specific example], we're looking for [simple outcome], not [elaborate approach they took]. Let's talk about how to identify when a task calls for a lighter touch versus deeper analysis."

What you're communicating: "You need to learn which tasks need a lot of work and which tasks need just a little. You're making simple, quick tasks way more complicated than they need to be. For [specific example], we just needed [simple outcome]—we didn't need you to do [all the extra stuff they did]. Let's figure out how you can tell when something should be quick and easy versus when it actually needs more work."

Breaking it down:

- **"I want to help you calibrate your approach for different types of assignments"** = "You need to learn how to match your effort to what each task actually needs"
- **"Tasks designed to be quick and straightforward are becoming more involved than they need to be"** = "You're making simple tasks way too complicated"
- **"For something like [specific example], we're looking for [simple outcome], not [elaborate approach they took]"** = "For [example], we just needed [simple thing], not [all the extra work you did]"
- **"Let's talk about how to identify when a task calls for a lighter touch versus deeper analysis"** = "Let's figure out how you can tell when to keep it simple versus when to dig deeper"

More Direct: "We need to address how you're allocating time and effort across tasks. You're treating assignments that require [X level of effort] as if they need [Y level of effort], and it's affecting your turnaround times. Not everything needs exhaustive analysis or detailed documentation. When I assign something with a tight deadline, that's a signal that we need sufficient quality quickly, not perfect quality slowly. You need to develop better judgment about when good enough is actually good enough."

What you're communicating: "You're spending way too much time and effort on tasks that don't need it. You're working on things that need [X amount of work] like they need [way more work], and it's making you slow. Not everything needs you to analyze it to death or document every detail. When I give you something and say it's due soon, that means I need it done reasonably well and fast—not done perfectly but slowly. You need to get better at knowing when something is good enough and you can stop working on it."

Breaking it down:

- **"We need to address how you're allocating time and effort across tasks"** = "We need to talk about how you're deciding how much work to put into different things"

- **"You're treating assignments that require [X level of effort] as if they need [Y level of effort]"** = "You're putting way more work into tasks than they actually need"
- **"And it's affecting your turnaround times"** = "And it's making you too slow"
- **"Not everything needs exhaustive analysis or detailed documentation"** = "Not everything needs you to analyze every detail or write everything down perfectly"
- **"When I assign something with a tight deadline, that's a signal"** = "When I tell you something is due soon, that should tell you something"
- **"That we need sufficient quality quickly—not perfect quality slowly"** = "That we need it done well enough and fast—not perfect but taking forever"
- **"You need to develop better judgment about when good enough is actually good enough"** = "You need to get better at knowing when to stop and call something done"

Firm: "I need to be clear about expectations: not every task warrants the same level of depth and detail. You're consistently overengineering simple assignments, and it's creating efficiency problems. When I provide a deadline and scope, those parameters are telling you how much effort the task merits. A task with a two-hour target doesn't need six hours of analysis. Learn to match your effort to the task requirements, or we're going to have ongoing problems with your productivity."

What you're communicating: "Let me be clear: different tasks need different amounts of work, and you need to understand that. You keep making simple tasks way more complicated than they should be, and it's making you too slow. When I tell you a deadline and what I need done, that should tell you how much work to put in. If something should take two hours, don't spend six hours analyzing it to death. Figure out how to match how much work you do to what the task actually needs, or we're going to keep having problems with you being too slow."

Breaking it down:

- **"I need to be clear about expectations"** = "Let me tell you exactly what I need from you"
- **"Not every task warrants the same level of depth and detail"** = "Different tasks need different amounts of work"
- **"You're consistently overengineering simple assignments"** = "You keep making easy tasks way more complicated than they need to be"
- **"And it's creating efficiency problems"** = "And it's making you too slow"
- **"When I provide a deadline and scope, those parameters are telling you how much effort the task merits"** = "When I tell you when it's due and what to do, that tells you how much work it should take"
- **"A task with a two-hour target doesn't need six hours of analysis"** = "If something should take two hours, don't spend six hours on it"
- **"Learn to match your effort to the task requirements"** = "Figure out how to put in the right amount of work for each task"
- **"Or we're going to have ongoing problems with your productivity"** = "Or you're going to keep being too slow and we'll keep having this problem"

Why This Works: You're identifying the specific problem—inability to right-size effort to task importance—without calling them clueless. The focus on "calibration" and "judgment" frames it as a skill to develop rather than a character flaw. The firm version makes it clear that over-complication isn't a sign of thoroughness; it's a productivity problem.

Scenario 4: Deadlines Are Treated as Suggestions

Situation: This employee consistently misses deadlines or asks for extensions at the last minute. They seem surprised when due dates arrive, as if they didn't know they were coming. There's always a reason—they underestimated the time needed, something "came up," they needed to perfect it—but the pattern is clear: deadlines don't seem to create any urgency for them.

What You're Thinking: "The deadline was three weeks away, and you're telling me the day before that you need more time? What exactly were you doing for the past 21 days? Did you think it would magically complete itself? Do you understand what a deadline actually means?"

What You Should Say:

Diplomatic: "I want to talk about timeline management. I've noticed that deadlines for [projects/tasks] have been challenging to meet consistently. When we set a due date, that's built into broader project planning, and other people's work depends on it. Let's discuss your process for managing toward deadlines—how you're breaking down work, tracking progress, and identifying when you're falling behind early enough to course-correct."

What you're communicating: "We need to talk about why you keep missing deadlines. You've been having trouble finishing things on time. When I give you a due date, that's not flexible—other people are counting on you to finish on time. Let's talk about how you manage your time on projects—how you break up the work, check if you're on track, and figure out early when you're running late so you can fix it before the deadline."

Breaking it down:

- **"I want to talk about timeline management"** = "We need to discuss why you keep missing deadlines"
- **"Deadlines for [projects/tasks] have been challenging to meet consistently"** = "You keep having trouble finishing things on time"
- **"When we set a due date, that's built into broader project planning"** = "When I give you a deadline, that affects other plans and projects"

- **"Other people's work depends on it"** = "Other people are counting on you to finish on time"
- **"Let's discuss your process for managing toward deadlines"** = "Let's talk about how you handle deadlines"
- **"How you're breaking down work, tracking progress"** = "How you split up the work and keep track of where you are"
- **"And identifying when you're falling behind early enough to course-correct"** = "And how you figure out early that you're running late so you can fix it"

More Direct: "We have a pattern of missed deadlines that we need to address. When I set a due date, that's not a suggestion—it's a commitment that affects project timelines and team coordination. You've missed [X] deadlines in the past [timeframe], and several others have required last-minute extensions. This tells me you're not accurately estimating time requirements or managing your work to meet commitments. Going forward, I need deadlines to be met as stated, or I need advance notice—not day-of notifications—that there's a problem."

What you're communicating: "You keep missing deadlines, and we need to fix this. When I give you a due date, that's not optional or flexible—it's a real deadline that affects other projects and what the team is doing. You've missed [X] deadlines in [timeframe], and you've asked to extend several others at the last minute. This tells me you're bad at figuring out how long things will take, or you're bad at managing your time to finish on schedule. From now on, you need to meet deadlines when I give them to you, or you need to tell me way ahead of time—not the day it's due—that there's a problem."

Breaking it down:

- **"We have a pattern of missed deadlines that we need to address"** = "You keep missing deadlines, and this is a problem we have to fix"
- **"When I set a due date, that's not a suggestion—it's a commitment"** = "When I give you a deadline, that's not optional—it's a real deadline"

- **"That affects project timelines and team coordination"** = "That impacts other projects and what the team needs to do"
- **"You've missed [X] deadlines in the past [timeframe]"** = "You've missed [X] deadlines recently"
- **"And several others have required last-minute extensions"** = "And you've asked to extend several others at the last second"
- **"This tells me you're not accurately estimating time requirements"** = "This shows me you're bad at figuring out how long things actually take"
- **"Or managing your work to meet commitments"** = "Or you're bad at managing your time to finish on schedule"
- **"I need deadlines to be met as stated"** = "You need to finish things by the deadline I give you"
- **"Or I need advance notice—not day-of notifications—that there's a problem"** = "Or you need to tell me way ahead of time, not the day it's due, that you won't make it"

Firm: "I need to be direct: your track record with deadlines has become a serious performance issue. Deadlines exist for a reason—they're not negotiable unless we discuss it well in advance. Missing them or requesting extensions at the last minute disrupts project flow and puts additional pressure on the rest of the team. I need to see a significant improvement in your ability to deliver on time. If you can't meet a deadline, I need to know at least [X days] in advance so we can adjust plans accordingly. Continued deadline issues will affect your performance evaluation."

What you're communicating: "Let me be blunt: you missing deadlines all the time is now a major problem with your job performance. Deadlines aren't optional—you can't just miss them or change them unless we talk about it way ahead of time. When you miss them or ask to extend them at the last minute, it messes up the whole project and makes things harder for everyone else on the team. You need to get a lot better at finishing things on time. If you can't make a deadline, you need to tell me at least [X days] early so we can change our plans. If you keep having deadline problems, it's going to hurt your performance review."

Breaking it down:

- **"I need to be direct: your track record with deadlines has become a serious performance issue"** = "Let me be clear: you missing deadlines is now a big problem with your job performance"
- **"Deadlines exist for a reason—they're not negotiable"** = "Deadlines are real and you can't just ignore them or change them"
- **"Unless we discuss it well in advance"** = "Unless we talk about it way ahead of time"
- **"Missing them or requesting extensions at the last minute disrupts project flow"** = "When you miss deadlines or ask to extend them at the last second, it messes up the whole project"
- **"And puts additional pressure on the rest of the team"** = "And makes things harder for everyone else"
- **"I need to see a significant improvement in your ability to deliver on time"** = "You need to get much better at finishing things by the deadline"
- **"If you can't meet a deadline, I need to know at least [X days] in advance"** = "If you're going to miss a deadline, tell me at least [X days] before it's due"
- **"So we can adjust plans accordingly"** = "So we can change our plans to deal with it"
- **"Continued deadline issues will affect your performance evaluation"** = "If you keep missing deadlines, it will hurt your performance review"

Why This Works: You're emphasizing that deadlines aren't arbitrary—they have downstream impacts. By focusing on the pattern rather than a single instance, you're making it clear this is a recurring problem. The firm version establishes consequences while still giving them a path forward (advance notice when problems arise).

Scenario 5: They're "Busy" But Produce Little

Situation: This employee always seems to be working—they're at their desk, they're in meetings, they talk about being swamped—but when you look at actual output, there's surprisingly little to show for all that activity. They're busy, but not productive. The motion doesn't match the results.

What You're Thinking: "You're always telling me how busy you are, but where's the work? Everyone else manages to produce deliverables. What exactly are you doing all day that looks like work but produces nothing? Are you just really good at looking busy?"

What You Should Say:

Diplomatic: "I want to make sure your time is being used effectively. I know you're putting in hours, but I'm not seeing that translate into proportional output. Let's look at how you're spending your time and where things might be getting stuck. Sometimes we can be busy with activities that aren't moving the needle on our actual priorities. Let's identify what's taking up time versus what's producing results, and reallocate accordingly."

What you're communicating: "I want to make sure you're actually getting things done with your time. I know you're working, but I'm not seeing you finish much, considering how much time you're putting in. Let's look at what you're doing all day and figure out where you're getting stuck or wasting time. Sometimes people stay busy doing things that don't actually matter or move work forward. Let's figure out what you're spending time on versus what's actually getting work done, and shift how you spend your time."

Breaking it down:

- **"I want to make sure your time is being used effectively"** = "I want to make sure you're actually accomplishing things"
- **"I know you're putting in hours"** = "I know you're working"
- **"But I'm not seeing that translate into proportional output"** =

"But you're not producing much considering how much time you're spending"

- **"Let's look at how you're spending your time and where things might be getting stuck"** = "Let's look at what you're doing all day and where you're wasting time or getting blocked"
- **"Sometimes we can be busy with activities that aren't moving the needle on our actual priorities"** = "Sometimes people stay busy doing stuff that doesn't actually matter"
- **"Let's identify what's taking up time versus what's producing results"** = "Let's figure out what you're spending time on versus what's actually getting work done"
- **"And reallocate accordingly"** = "And change how you use your time"

More Direct: "We need to talk about productivity. There's a disconnect between activity level and output. Being busy isn't the same as being productive, and right now I'm seeing a lot of motion but not enough completed deliverables. I need you to shift focus from staying busy to delivering results. That might mean saying no to low-value activities, streamlining your process, or being more strategic about where you invest time. The measure of success here is what you complete, not how many hours you appear to be working."

What you're communicating: "We need to discuss how much you're actually getting done. You seem busy, but you're not producing much. Being busy and being productive aren't the same thing, and right now, you're moving around a lot but not finishing enough actual work. You need to stop focusing on staying busy and start focusing on finishing things. That might mean you have to stop doing unimportant stuff, find faster ways to work, or be smarter about what you spend time on. What matters is what you actually finish, not how busy you look."

Breaking it down:

- **"We need to talk about productivity"** = "We need to discuss how much you're actually getting done"

- **"There's a disconnect between activity level and output"** = "You seem busy but you're not producing much"
- **"Being busy isn't the same as being productive"** = "Looking busy and actually getting things done are different"
- **"Right now I'm seeing a lot of motion but not enough completed deliverables"** = "Right now you're moving around a lot but not finishing enough work"
- **"I need you to shift focus from staying busy to delivering results"** = "Stop worrying about looking busy and start focusing on actually finishing things"
- **"That might mean saying no to low-value activities"** = "That might mean you stop doing unimportant stuff"
- **"Streamlining your process"** = "Finding faster ways to work"
- **"Or being more strategic about where you invest time"** = "Or being smarter about what you spend time on"
- **"The measure of success here is what you complete, not how many hours you appear to be working"** = "What matters is what you finish, not how busy you look"

Firm: "I need to address a performance concern: your output doesn't match your reported workload. You consistently describe being busy, yet deliverables aren't meeting the expected volume or timeliness. This suggests either a significant efficiency problem or a misalignment of priorities. Going forward, we'll be tracking specific deliverables and completion rates, not just activity. I need to see measurable improvement in what you're producing. If there are legitimate obstacles preventing productivity, we need to identify and address them now."

What you're communicating: "I have a serious concern about your performance: you say you're busy all the time, but you're not producing enough work or finishing things on time. This means either you're very inefficient at getting work done, or you're spending time on the wrong things. From now on, we're going to track exactly what you finish and how much you complete, not just whether you seem busy. You need to produce noticeably more work. If there are real problems stopping you from being productive, we need to find them and fix them right now."

Breaking it down:

- **"I need to address a performance concern"** = "I have a serious problem with your job performance to discuss"
- **"Your output doesn't match your reported workload"** = "You say you're busy, but you're not producing enough"
- **"You consistently describe being busy, yet deliverables aren't meeting expected volume or timeliness"** = "You always say you're swamped, but you're not finishing enough or finishing on time"
- **"This suggests either a significant efficiency problem or a misalignment of priorities"** = "This means you're either really bad at working efficiently, or you're working on the wrong things"
- **"Going forward, we'll be tracking specific deliverables and completion rates, not just activity"** = "From now on, we're measuring exactly what you finish, not just whether you look busy"
- **"I need to see measurable improvement in what you're producing"** = "You need to produce noticeably more work"
- **"If there are legitimate obstacles preventing productivity, we need to identify and address them now"** = "If real problems are stopping you from getting work done, we need to find them and fix them right now"

Why This Works: You're distinguishing between activity and productivity without accusing them of slacking off. By focusing on output metrics rather than perceived effort, you're making the conversation objective. The firm version establishes that you'll be measuring results going forward, which creates accountability.

Scenario 6: Basic Tasks Require Extraordinary Time

Situation: Simple, routine tasks that are foundational to the role consistently take this employee an unreasonable amount of time. These aren't complex projects—they're basic job functions that should be almost automatic by now. Yet they're still laboring over them as if each one is brand new.

What You're Thinking: "This is literally a core function of your job that you do every week. How are you still taking this long? This should be almost automatic for you by now. Do you reset your brain every weekend and forget everything you learned?"

What You Should Say:

Diplomatic: "I want to help you build efficiency on [routine task]. This is something you're doing regularly, and my expectation is that repetition should be making it faster and more automatic. Instead, I'm seeing it still requires significant time. Let's look at whether there are tools, templates, or process improvements that could streamline this for you, because you should be finding this much easier than you seem to be."

What you're communicating: "I want to help you get faster at [routine task]. You do this all the time, so I expected you'd be getting faster and finding it easier with practice. But you're not—it still takes you a long time. Let's see if there are shortcuts, templates, or better ways to do this that could speed you up, because you should be finding this much easier by now than you seem to."

Breaking it down:

- **"I want to help you build efficiency on [routine task]"** = "I want to help you get faster at this task you do all the time"
- **"This is something you're doing regularly"** = "You do this task often"
- **"And my expectation is that repetition should be making it faster and more automatic"** = "So I expected practice would make you faster and make it feel easier"
- **"Instead, I'm seeing it still requires significant time"** = "But it still takes you way too long"
- **"Let's look at whether there are tools, templates, or process improvements that could streamline this"** = "Let's see if there are shortcuts or better ways to do this that would speed you up"

- **"Because you should be finding this much easier than you seem to be"** = "Because this should feel a lot easier to you by now than it seems to"

More Direct: "We need to address your turnaround time on [routine task]. This is a regular responsibility that you should have down to a system by now. The fact that it's still taking [X time] when it should take [Y time] indicates either a process problem or a capability concern. I need you to develop a more efficient approach to this task—this isn't something that should still be challenging, given your time here."

What you're communicating: "We need to fix how long it takes you to do [routine task]. This is something you do regularly and should have figured out by now. The fact that it still takes you [X time] when it should only take [Y time] means either you're doing it the wrong way or you're just not capable of getting faster. You need to find a faster way to do this—you've been doing this long enough that it shouldn't still be hard for you."

Breaking it down:

- **"We need to address your turnaround time on [routine task]"** = "We need to fix how long this regular task takes you"
- **"This is a regular responsibility that you should have down to a system by now"** = "You do this all the time, so you should have figured out an efficient way to do it"
- **"The fact that it's still taking [X time] when it should take [Y time]"** = "The fact that it takes you [X time] when it should only take [Y time]"
- **"Indicates either a process problem or a capability concern"** = "Means either you're doing it wrong or you're just not able to get faster"
- **"I need you to develop a more efficient approach to this task"** = "You need to find a faster way to do this"
- **"This isn't something that should still be challenging at your tenure"** = "You've been here long enough that this shouldn't still be hard"

Firm: "I need to be direct about a performance issue with [routine task]. This is a fundamental part of your role, and the time you're spending on it is significantly above what's reasonable for someone with your experience. This should be one of your most efficient tasks by now, but it's become a bottleneck. I need to see your completion time for this cut to [reasonable timeframe] within the next [timeframe]. If you're unclear on how to achieve that, we need to discuss it, because this level of productivity on a core task isn't sustainable."

What you're communicating: "Let me be blunt about a problem with your performance on [routine task]. This is a basic part of your job, and you're taking way longer on it than makes sense for someone who's been doing it as long as you have. This should be one of the fastest, easiest things you do, but instead it's slowing everything down. You need to get your time on this down to [reasonable time] within [time-frame]. If you don't know how to get that fast, we need to talk about it, because you're taking this long on such a basic task, and can't continue."

Breaking it down:

- **"I need to be direct about a performance issue with [routine task]"** = "Let me be clear about a problem with how you do this regular task"
- **"This is a fundamental part of your role"** = "This is a basic part of your job"
- **"And the time you're spending on it is significantly above what's reasonable"** = "And you're taking way longer than you should"
- **"For someone with your experience"** = "For someone who's been doing this as long as you have"
- **"This should be one of your most efficient tasks by now"** = "This should be one of the fastest, easiest things you do"
- **"But it's become a bottleneck"** = "But instead it's slowing everything down"
- **"I need to see your completion time for this cut to**

[reasonable timeframe] within the next [timeframe]" = "You need to get this done in [reasonable time] by [timeframe]"

- **"If you're unclear on how to achieve that, we need to discuss it"** = "If you don't know how to work that fast, we need to talk about it"
- **"Because this level of productivity on a core task isn't sustainable"** = "Because you taking this long on such a basic task can't keep happening"

Why This Works: You're highlighting the disconnect between task frequency and completion time—the fact that practice hasn't led to improvement. By calling it a "routine task" or "fundamental part of your role," you're emphasizing this isn't exotic work that should be difficult. The firm version makes it clear that slow performance on basic tasks is a serious issue.

HR-APPROVED PHRASE COLLECTION

Instead of "You're too slow"

A. "We need to discuss turnaround times for [task type]."
B. "I'm seeing completion times that exceed our benchmarks."
C. "Your pace on [task] isn't matching team standards."
D. "We need to work on efficiency for [type of work]."
E. "The timeline for this work isn't sustainable."
F. "Let's talk about ways to streamline your process."
G. "I need to see faster turnaround on these assignments."
H. "Your completion rate is below what we need for this role."

Instead of "This shouldn't take you this long"

A. "This task typically takes [X timeframe]—let's discuss what's extending yours."
B. "The standard completion time for this is [X]—I'm seeing [Y] from you."

C. "Most team members complete this in [timeframe]."
D. "This level of work usually takes [X]—help me understand what's different in your case."
E. "We have a benchmark of [X] for this task."
F. "The time investment here seems disproportionate to the scope."

Instead of "Everyone else is faster than you"

A. "Let's align your completion times with team benchmarks."
B. "Your turnaround is significantly longer than the standard for this work."
C. "We need to bring your pace in line with team expectations."
D. "The typical completion time for this role is [X]."
E. "Other team members are completing this in [timeframe]."
F. "I need you working at the pace this position requires."

Instead of "Stop asking me to hold your hand"

A. "I want to help you build more independence on this task."
B. "You should be able to execute this without step-by-step guidance at this point."
C. "Let's work on reducing the oversight needed for routine tasks."
D. "I need you to take more ownership of this process."
E. "You've completed this enough times that you should be able to work through it independently."
F. "The level of guidance you're requiring isn't appropriate for your experience level with this."
G. "I expect you to work through routine tasks on your own."

Instead of "You're overcomplicating everything"

A. "This task doesn't require the level of analysis you're applying."
B. "We need to right-size your effort to the task at hand."

C. "Not every assignment needs exhaustive detail."
D. "Learn to distinguish between tasks that need depth and those that need speed."
E. "You're treating this as more complex than it needs to be."
F. "This calls for a lighter touch than you're giving it."
G. "We need sufficient quality quickly, not perfect quality slowly."
H. "Good enough is acceptable here—perfect isn't necessary."

Instead of "You missed the deadline again"

A. "We have a pattern of missed deadlines we need to address."
B. "Meeting deadlines needs to be a higher priority."
C. "I need to see improvement in your ability to deliver on time."
D. "Deadlines aren't suggestions—they're commitments."
E. "Your track record with timelines has become a concern."
F. "We need to discuss why deadlines have been challenging to meet."
G. "I need advance notice if you can't meet a deadline, not day-of notifications."

Instead of "You're busy but produce nothing"

A. "There's a disconnect between activity level and output."
B. "Being busy isn't the same as being productive."
C. "I need to see your time translate into deliverables."
D. "Your output doesn't match your reported workload."
E. "Let's focus on completed work rather than time spent."
F. "We need to look at what you're producing versus what you're working on."
G. "The measure of success is what you complete, not how many hours you work."

Instead of "You lack urgency"

A. "I need to see more responsiveness when deadlines are tight."

B. "This needs to be treated as a priority."
C. "The pace here needs to reflect the timeline we're working against."
D. "I'm not seeing appropriate urgency on time-sensitive work."
E. "When something is marked urgent, that needs to be reflected in your turnaround."
F. "This deadline requires you to accelerate your pace."

Instead of "You're inefficient"

A. "Let's look at ways to streamline your process."
B. "There are efficiency gains we need to find here."
C. "We need to identify where time is being lost in your workflow."
D. "Your approach could benefit from optimization."
E. "Let's find a more efficient path to the same outcome."
F. "There's an opportunity to work smarter, not just harder, on this."

Instead of "You waste time"

A. "Let's ensure your time is being allocated to high-value activities."
B. "We need to be more strategic about where you invest effort."
C. "Some activities may not be worth the time they're consuming."
D. "Let's prioritize tasks that move the needle on our goals."
E. "We should reallocate time from [lower value] to [higher value activities]."

Instead of "You're dragging down the team"

A. "Your pace is impacting overall team capacity."
B. "This is affecting what we can commit to as a team."

C. "The timeline here is creating downstream effects on other projects."
D. "Your turnaround time is becoming a bottleneck for the team."
E. "This affects our collective ability to meet commitments."

For setting clear expectations about speed

A. "For this type of work, I expect a turnaround of [X timeframe]."
B. "Going forward, these assignments should take no more than [X time]."
C. "The benchmark for this task is [X]—that's what I need you working toward."
D. "I need you to be able to complete [X number] of these per [timeframe]."
E. "Your target productivity should be [specific metric]."
F. "Let's establish clear time expectations for your routine tasks."

When they make excuses about timing

A. "Let's discuss how to build more accurate time estimates into your planning."
B. "I need you to account for these factors when committing to deadlines."
C. "If you consistently need more time than allocated, we have a planning problem to solve."
D. "These reasons are becoming a pattern—we need to address the root cause."
E. "I need you to flag timeline concerns earlier in the process."

For distinguishing between speed and quality

A. "Speed shouldn't come at the expense of quality, but quality shouldn't come at the expense of timeliness."
B. "We need both acceptable quality and appropriate speed."
C. "The goal is to work efficiently while maintaining standards."

D. "I need you to find the balance between thorough and timely."
E. "Perfection is the enemy of progress here."

Chapter 2 Quick Reference Box

Ten Essential Phrases for Slow Workers & Low Productivity

1. "Your completion times are significantly exceeding benchmarks—let's discuss what's driving that."

2. "We need to address the pattern of missed deadlines. They're commitments, not suggestions."

3. "At this point in your experience with this task, you should be able to execute it independently."

4. "There's a disconnect between activity level and output. Let's focus on what you're completing."

5. "Not every task requires the same level of detail. Learn to right-size your effort to the assignment."

6. "The time you're spending on routine tasks is significantly above what's reasonable for your experience level."

7. "I need you working at the pace this position requires, which is [specific benchmark]."

8. "Let's identify where time is being lost in your workflow so we can find efficiency gains."

9. "When I provide a deadline, that tells you how much effort the task merits. Match your work to those parameters."

10. "I need to see measurable improvement in your turnaround times within [timeframe], or this becomes a serious performance issue."

QUICK FAVOR: HELP ANOTHER MANAGER

You're halfway through this book, which means you've already found some phrases you needed. If they've helped, would you be so kind as to take 30 seconds to leave a quick review?

Why? Because right now, some manager is searching Amazon in the middle of the night, dreading tomorrow's conversation, wondering if this book will actually help.

Your review—even just "These phrases work" or "Wish I'd found this sooner"—tells them this isn't another useless management theory book.

Scan the QR code to leave a quick Amazon review:

Then get back to finding the language for your next difficult conversation.

Thanks.

—The HR Approved Ways Team

THREE

WHEN THEY DON'T GET IT (COMPREHENSION ISSUES)

"Let's Make Sure We're Aligned"
(Translation: You're Not Understanding This)

Real Talk

There's a special kind of frustration that comes from explaining something for the fifth time and watching the person nod along like they understand when you know—you absolutely know—they still don't get it. You've explained it clearly. You've used examples. You've walked them through it step by step. And yet here they are, coming back with the same confused questions or producing work that proves they completely missed the point.

Maybe they're not grasping the underlying concepts. Maybe they're misinterpreting instructions in ways that make no logical sense. Maybe they're solving for the wrong problem entirely because they can't seem to understand what you're actually asking for. Or maybe they just lack the critical thinking skills to connect the dots that seem obvious to everyone else.

The worst part? They often think they understand. They'll confidently nod, say "got it," and then go do something that demonstrates they absolutely did not get it. And you're left wondering: Is this a communication problem on my end? Is this a listening problem on their end? Or is this just a fundamental gap in their ability to process information?

You obviously can't say "are you dense?" or "how are you not understanding this?" or "this is simple and you're making it complicated." But you also can't keep re-explaining basic concepts indefinitely when everyone else grasped them immediately. This chapter gives you the language to address comprehension issues without making it about intelligence or making someone feel stupid.

Five Principles for the 'You're Not Getting This' Conversation

- **Start with questions, not accusations.** "Walk me through your understanding of X" reveals the gap without saying "you don't understand."

- **Separate the concept from the person.** The problem is "a gap in understanding" or "misalignment on the concept," not "you're not smart enough."

- **Use multiple approaches to explain.** If they didn't get it the first way, try a different angle—example, analogy, visual. If they still don't get it after three attempts, that's when it becomes a performance conversation.

- **Document the pattern.** One misunderstanding is normal. Repeated comprehension issues on the same or similar concepts indicate a bigger problem that needs to be addressed.

- **Be direct about the impact.** When lack of comprehension leads to mistakes, missed objectives, or wasted time, make that connection explicit so they understand why this matters.

Let's Get Real Scenarios

Scenario 1: You've Explained This Five Times

Situation: You've explained a process, concept, or task requirement multiple times now. Each time, the employee nods, says they understand, and then asks the same questions again or demonstrates through their work that they still don't grasp it. You're running out of ways to explain the same thing, and it's eating up your time.

What You're Thinking: "How many different ways can I explain this? Everyone else got it the first time. Are you even listening? Do you forget everything the moment you walk away? Why do you keep asking me the exact same questions?"

What You Should Say:

Diplomatic: "I want to make sure we have clarity on [concept/process]. We've discussed this a few times, and I'm still seeing questions that suggest there might be some confusion. Let's try a different approach—can you walk me through your understanding of how this works? That will help me identify where the disconnect is so I can explain it more effectively."

What you're communicating: "You still don't understand this, even though we've talked about it multiple times. Your questions show you're confused. Let me hear you explain it back to me so I can figure out what part you're not getting, because clearly my explanations aren't working."

Breaking it down:

- **"I want to make sure we have clarity on [concept/process]"** = "I need to know if you actually understand this"

- **"We've discussed this a few times"** = "I've explained this to you multiple times already"
- **"And I'm still seeing questions that suggest there might be some confusion"** = "Your questions prove you still don't get it"
- **"Let's try a different approach"** = "Since my explanations haven't worked so far"
- **"Can you walk me through your understanding of how this works?"** = "Explain it back to me so I can see what you're missing"
- **"That will help me identify where the disconnect is"** = "So I can figure out which part you're not understanding"
- **"So I can explain it more effectively"** = "So I can try yet another way of explaining this to you"

More Direct: "We need to address a pattern I'm seeing with [concept/process]. I've explained this multiple times, and you're still asking the same fundamental questions. This tells me the information isn't sticking, or there's a gap in understanding we haven't resolved. I need you to be honest with me: what specifically about this is unclear? Because we can't keep revisiting the same ground repeatedly."

What you're communicating: "There's a problem with how you keep not understanding [concept/process]. I've explained this many times, and you keep asking the same basic questions. This means either you're not remembering what I tell you, or you don't understand something fundamental. Tell me honestly what you don't understand, because I can't keep explaining the same thing over and over."

Breaking it down:

- **"We need to address a pattern I'm seeing"** = "This keeps happening and it's a problem"
- **"I've explained this multiple times"** = "I've already told you this several times"
- **"And you're still asking the same fundamental questions"** = "But you keep asking the same basic questions"
- **"This tells me the information isn't sticking or there's a gap in understanding"** = "This means you're either not remembering or not understanding"
- **"We haven't resolved"** = "That we still haven't fixed"
- **"I need you to be honest with me: what specifically about this is unclear?"** = "Tell me straight up: what part don't you understand?"
- **"Because we can't keep revisiting the same ground repeatedly"** = "Because I can't keep explaining the same thing over and over"

Firm: "I need to be direct about a concern. We've covered [concept/process] multiple times now, and you're continuing to struggle with the same elements. At this point, the issue isn't that I haven't explained it clearly—it's that the concept isn't taking hold. I need you to invest serious effort into understanding this, whether that means taking detailed notes, reviewing documentation on your own time, or finding additional resources. This is a core requirement of your role, and the repeated confusion is becoming a performance issue."

What you're communicating: "Let me be blunt about a problem. I've explained [concept/process] to you many times, and you're still struggling with the same basic parts. By now, the problem isn't that I'm not explaining it well—it's that you're not grasping it. You need to work hard to understand this, whether that means writing everything down, studying on your own, or finding other ways to learn it. This is something you must understand for your job, and you keep not understanding it, which is now a serious performance problem."

Breaking it down:

- **"I need to be direct about a concern"** = "I'm going to be blunt about a problem"
- **"We've covered [concept/process] multiple times now"** = "I've explained this to you many times"
- **"And you're continuing to struggle with the same elements"** = "But you still don't understand the same basic parts"
- **"At this point, the issue isn't that I haven't explained it clearly"** = "By now, it's not that my explanations are bad"
- **"It's that the concept isn't taking hold"** = "It's that you're not grasping it"
- **"I need you to invest serious effort into understanding this"** = "You need to work really hard to learn this"
- **"Whether that means taking detailed notes, reviewing documentation on your own time, or finding additional resources"** = "Like writing everything down, studying when you're not at work, or finding other ways to learn"
- **"This is a core requirement of your role"** = "This is something you have to know for your job"
- **"The repeated confusion is becoming a performance issue"** = "You keep not understanding it, and that's now a serious problem with your job performance"

Why This Works: The diplomatic version opens the possibility that you need to explain differently, which gives them an out while still surfacing the problem. The direct version makes it clear this is a pattern that needs to stop. The firm version establishes that repeated failure to grasp fundamental concepts is a capability issue, not just a communication hiccup.

Scenario 2: They're Solving for the Wrong Problem Entirely

Situation: You assign a task with a clear objective, and the employee comes back with work that addresses a completely different issue. It's not that they did it poorly—they solved the wrong problem. They fundamentally misunderstood what you were asking for, and now you've lost time to work that's entirely off-target.

What You're Thinking: "How did you get from what I said to what you did? We weren't even in the same universe. Were you listening at all? Did you just hear random words and decide to do whatever you felt like? This isn't even close to what I asked for."

What You Should Say:

Diplomatic: "I think we got our wires crossed on the objective here. Looking at what you've produced, I can see you put effort into solving for [what they did], but what we actually needed was [what you wanted]. Let's back up and make sure we're aligned on the problem we're trying to solve before you continue. Can you articulate back to me what the core issue is that we're addressing?"

What you're communicating: "We had a miscommunication about what you were supposed to do. I can see you worked on [wrong thing], but we actually needed [right thing]. Let's stop and make sure you understand what problem we're actually trying to fix before you do more work. Tell me in your own words what the main issue is that we're working on."

Breaking it down:

- **"I think we got our wires crossed on the objective here"** = "You misunderstood what you were supposed to do"
- **"Looking at what you've produced, I can see you put effort into solving for [what they did]"** = "I can see you worked on [wrong thing]"
- **"But what we actually needed was [what you wanted]"** = "But we actually needed [completely different thing]"
- **"Let's back up and make sure we're aligned on the problem we're trying to solve"** = "Let's stop and make sure you understand what we're actually trying to fix"
- **"Before you continue"** = "Before you waste more time on the wrong thing"
- **"Can you articulate back to me what the core issue is that we're addressing?"** = "Tell me what you think the main problem is that we're working on"

More Direct: "There's a significant disconnect between what I asked for and what you delivered. I asked you to address [X], and what you've produced addresses [Y] instead. This suggests you misunderstood the fundamental objective. Before we move forward, I need to ensure you understand what problem we're actually solving and why. This kind of misalignment costs us significant time and resources."

What you're communicating: "There's a big gap between what I asked for and what you did. I asked you to work on [X], and you worked on [Y] instead. This shows you didn't understand the basic goal. Before we do anything else, I need to make sure you know what we're actually trying to do and why it matters. When you work on the wrong thing, it wastes a lot of time and money."

Breaking it down:

- **"There's a significant disconnect between what I asked for and what you delivered"** = "What you did is very different from what I asked you to do"
- **"I asked you to address [X], and what you've produced addresses [Y] instead"** = "I asked for [X] but you did [Y]"
- **"This suggests you misunderstood the fundamental objective"** = "This shows you didn't understand the basic goal"
- **"Before we move forward, I need to ensure you understand what problem we're actually solving and why"** = "Before we continue, I need to make sure you know what we're really trying to do and why"
- **"This kind of misalignment costs us significant time and resources"** = "When you work on the wrong thing, it wastes a lot of time and money"

Firm: "We have a serious problem. The work you've delivered addresses an entirely different issue than what was requested. This isn't a matter of execution—you solved for the wrong problem. That indicates either you didn't understand the assignment or you didn't seek clarification when you should have. Either way, this is a significant miss that we can't afford to repeat. Going forward, if you're unclear on the objective, you need to ask before investing time and effort in the wrong direction."

What you're communicating: "This is a major problem. The work you did is for a completely different issue than what I asked for. This isn't about doing it badly—you worked on the wrong problem entirely. This means either you didn't understand what I asked you to do, or you didn't ask questions when you should have. No matter what, this is a big mistake that can't happen again. From now on, if you don't understand what I want, you need to ask me before you spend time working on the wrong thing."

Breaking it down:

- **"We have a serious problem"** = "This is a major issue"
- **"The work you've delivered addresses an entirely different issue than what was requested"** = "What you did is for a completely different problem than what I asked for"
- **"This isn't a matter of execution—you solved for the wrong problem"** = "This isn't about doing it badly—you worked on the wrong problem completely"
- **"That indicates either you didn't understand the assignment or you didn't seek clarification when you should have"** = "This means either you didn't understand what I asked or you didn't ask questions when you were confused"
- **"Either way, this is a significant miss that we can't afford to repeat"** = "No matter what caused it, this is a big mistake that can't happen again"
- **"Going forward, if you're unclear on the objective, you need to ask before investing time and effort in the wrong direction"** = "From now on, if you don't understand what I want, ask me before you waste time working on the wrong thing"

Why This Works: You're acknowledging effort while making it clear the direction was completely off. By asking them to articulate the problem back to you, you're testing comprehension without making it feel like a quiz. The firm version makes it clear that solving for the wrong problem is a serious issue that suggests either comprehension problems or poor judgment about when to ask for help.

Scenario 3: Basic Cause-and-Effect Escapes Them

Situation: The employee consistently fails to understand logical connections or consequences. They can't seem to grasp that if A happens, B will follow. They're surprised by predictable outcomes and don't anticipate obvious next steps. It's not about complex analysis—it's basic "if this, then that" reasoning.

What You're Thinking: "How do you not see that connection? A five-year-old could follow this logic. If you do X, obviously Y is going to happen. Why are you shocked by this completely predictable result? Do you just not think things through at all?"

What You Should Say:

Diplomatic: "I want to talk about how we're thinking through consequences and next steps. I'm noticing situations where the connection between [action] and [result] isn't being anticipated. For example, when [specific instance], the outcome was fairly predictable based on [cause]. Let's work on building that analytical muscle—thinking through what's likely to happen as a result of certain actions or decisions."

What you're communicating: "We need to discuss how you think about what happens next and what causes what. I'm seeing that you don't predict the connection between [action] and [result]. Like when [specific example], what happened should have been obvious because of [cause]. You need to get better at thinking through what will probably happen because of certain actions or choices."

Breaking it down:

- **"I want to talk about how we're thinking through consequences and next steps"** = "We need to discuss how you predict what will happen next"

- **"I'm noticing situations where the connection between [action] and [result] isn't being anticipated"** = "I'm seeing that you don't expect [action] to cause [result]"
- **"For example, when [specific instance], the outcome was fairly predictable based on [cause]"** = "Like when [specific example], what happened should have been obvious because of [cause]"
- **"Let's work on building that analytical muscle"** = "You need to get better at this kind of thinking"
- **"Thinking through what's likely to happen as a result of certain actions or decisions"** = "Figuring out what will probably happen because of what you do or choose"

More Direct: "We need to address a pattern in how you're approaching problems. You're not consistently thinking through cause and effect or anticipating logical consequences. When [X] happened, the result was [Y]—that's a direct and predictable connection that should have been obvious. I need you to slow down and think through the chain of events: if I do this, what's likely to happen next? This kind of logical reasoning is essential for your role."

What you're communicating: "There's a problem with how you approach problems. You're not thinking about what causes what or predicting obvious results. When [X] happened and caused [Y], that connection was direct and predictable, and you should have seen it coming. You need to take more time to think through what happens next: if I do this, what will probably happen? This kind of logical thinking is necessary for your job."

Breaking it down:

- **"We need to address a pattern in how you're approaching**

problems" = "There's a problem with how you deal with problems"

- **"You're not consistently thinking through cause and effect or anticipating logical consequences"** = "You're not thinking about what causes what or predicting obvious results"

- **"When [X] happened, the result was [Y]—that's a direct and predictable connection"** = "When [X] caused [Y]—that was a direct connection"

- **"That should have been obvious"** = "You should have seen that coming"

- **"I need you to slow down and think through the chain of events: if I do this, what's likely to happen next?"** = "You need to take time to think about what happens next: if I do this, what will probably happen?"

- **"This kind of logical reasoning is essential for your role"** = "This type of thinking is required for your job"

Firm: "I need to be direct about a critical gap I'm seeing. You're repeatedly missing cause-and-effect relationships that are fundamental to good decision-making. The inability to anticipate logical consequences or connect actions to outcomes is causing mistakes that could be avoided with basic critical thinking. This isn't about complex analysis—this is about straightforward reasoning that's essential for this position. I need to see marked improvement in your ability to think through scenarios and anticipate results."

What you're communicating: "Let me be blunt about a serious problem I'm seeing. You keep missing obvious cause-and-effect connections that are basic to making good decisions. Not being able to predict logical results or see how actions lead to outcomes is causing avoidable mistakes. This isn't about complicated analysis—this is about simple reasoning that you must have for this job. You need to get much better at thinking through situations and predicting what will happen."

Breaking it down:

- **"I need to be direct about a critical gap I'm seeing"** = "Let me be blunt about a serious problem I see"
- **"You're repeatedly missing cause-and-effect relationships that are fundamental to good decision-making"** = "You keep missing obvious connections between causes and effects that are basic to making good decisions"
- **"The inability to anticipate logical consequences or connect actions to outcomes"** = "Not being able to predict obvious results or see how actions lead to outcomes"
- **"Is causing mistakes that could be avoided with basic critical thinking"** = "Is causing mistakes that wouldn't happen if you used simple reasoning"
- **"This isn't about complex analysis—this is about straightforward reasoning"** = "This isn't about complicated thinking—this is about simple logic"
- **"That's essential for this position"** = "That you must have for this job"
- **"I need to see marked improvement in your ability to think through scenarios and anticipate results"** = "You need to get much better at thinking through situations and predicting what will happen"

Why This Works: You're identifying a specific type of thinking deficit (cause-and-effect reasoning) without saying "you're not smart." By using concrete examples, you're showing them exactly where the gap is. The firm version makes it clear that this isn't an optional skillset—it's a fundamental requirement for the role.

Scenario 4: They Keep Asking Questions You Already Answered

Situation: You explain something, answer their questions thoroughly, and then—sometimes within the same conversation—they ask you questions you literally just answered. It's not a memory issue with old information; they're not retaining what you said five minutes ago.

What You're Thinking: "I just told you that. I literally just said that exact thing. Were you not listening? Were you thinking about lunch? Do words just bounce off your brain without leaving any impression? How can you ask me something I answered two minutes ago?"

What You Should Say:

Diplomatic: "I want to make sure information is landing effectively when we talk. I'm noticing that sometimes questions come up that we've already covered in the same conversation. That suggests maybe I'm not explaining clearly enough, or there's too much information at once. When we discuss something, could you take notes so you have a reference? And if something I say doesn't make sense, stop me right then so we can clarify before moving on."

What you're communicating: "I need to make sure you're actually understanding me when I talk. I'm seeing that you sometimes ask questions about things I just explained in the same conversation. This might mean I'm not explaining well, or I'm giving you too much information at once. When we talk about something, can you write things down so you can look back at them? And if you don't understand something I say, interrupt me right away so we can fix it before continuing."

Breaking it down:

- **"I want to make sure information is landing effectively when we talk"** = "I need to know you're actually understanding me when I explain things"
- **"I'm noticing that sometimes questions come up that we've already covered in the same conversation"** = "You sometimes ask about things I just explained moments ago"
- **"That suggests maybe I'm not explaining clearly enough, or there's too much information at once"** = "This might mean I'm confusing or overwhelming you"
- **"When we discuss something, could you take notes so you have a reference?"** = "Can you write things down when I explain them?"
- **"And if something I say doesn't make sense, stop me right then so we can clarify before moving on"** = "If you don't understand something, interrupt me immediately so we can fix it"

MORE DIRECT: "We have a communication issue we need to address. You're asking questions about information I've already provided in the same conversation. This is happening frequently enough that it's a pattern. I need you to actively focus when we're discussing something important—that means putting away distractions, taking notes, and asking for clarification in the moment if something's unclear. I can't repeat the same information multiple times in one conversation."

What you're communicating: "There's a communication problem we need to fix. You're asking about things I already told you in the same conversation. This happens often enough that it's a real pattern. You need to really pay attention when we're talking about important things —that means no distractions, write things down, and ask questions right away if you're confused. I can't keep repeating myself within the same conversation."

Breaking it down:

- **"We have a communication issue we need to address"** = "There's a communication problem we have to fix"
- **"You're asking questions about information I've already provided in the same conversation"** = "You're asking about things I just told you"
- **"This is happening frequently enough that it's a pattern"** = "This happens enough that it's a regular problem"
- **"I need you to actively focus when we're discussing something important"** = "You need to really concentrate when we talk about important things"
- **"That means putting away distractions, taking notes, and asking for clarification in the moment"** = "That means no distractions, write things down, and ask questions right away"
- **"If something's unclear"** = "If you're confused"
- **"I can't repeat the same information multiple times in one conversation"** = "I can't keep saying the same thing over and over in one discussion"

Firm: "I need to be direct about something that's becoming a significant issue. You're regularly asking questions about things I've just explained in the same conversation. This indicates either you're not listening attentively or information isn't being processed and retained. Either way, it's creating inefficiency and frustration. Going forward, when we have important discussions, I need your full attention, and I need you to take responsibility for capturing the information. If you're unclear about something, ask immediately—but I can't continue re-explaining things I've already covered in the same discussion."

What you're communicating: "Let me be direct about something that's becoming a real problem. You keep asking about things I just explained moments ago. This means either you're not paying attention or you're not processing and remembering what I say. Whatever the reason, it's wasting time and frustrating me. From now on, when we have important conversations, you need to focus completely, and you need to make sure you capture the information. If something's confusing, ask right away—but I can't keep repeating things I already said in the same conversation."

Breaking it down:

- **"I need to be direct about something that's becoming a significant issue"** = "Let me be blunt about a problem that's getting serious"
- **"You're regularly asking questions about things I've just explained in the same conversation"** = "You keep asking about things I just told you moments ago"
- **"This indicates either you're not listening attentively or information isn't being processed and retained"** = "This means either you're not paying attention or you're not understanding and remembering"
- **"Either way, it's creating inefficiency and frustration"** = "No matter the reason, it's wasting time and annoying me"
- **"Going forward, when we have important discussions, I need your full attention"** = "From now on, when we talk about important things, you need to focus completely"

- **"And I need you to take responsibility for capturing the information"** = "And you need to make sure you capture what I'm telling you"
- **"If you're unclear about something, ask immediately"** = "If something confuses you, ask right away"
- **"But I can't continue re-explaining things I've already covered in the same discussion"** = "But I can't keep repeating what I already said in the same conversation"

Why This Works: The diplomatic version assumes positive intent and offers solutions (note-taking, real-time clarification). The direct version names the pattern and sets clear expectations for attention and retention. The firm version makes it explicit that this is unacceptable and puts the responsibility on them to capture and process information effectively.

Scenario 5: They Misinterpret Clear Instructions

Situation: You give straightforward, unambiguous instructions, and somehow they interpret them in a way that makes no sense. It's not that the instructions were vague—they were crystal clear. But they've added assumptions, ignored key words, or twisted the meaning into something entirely different from what you said.

What You're Thinking: "How did you read that and think it meant this? The words I used have actual definitions. I didn't say anything that could be interpreted this way. Are you just making stuff up? Do you read into everything that isn't there?"

What You Should Say:

Diplomatic: "I want to make sure we're interpreting instructions the same way. When I said [exact instruction], you understood that to mean [what they did]. Can you walk me through your thought process there? I'm trying to understand how we got from what I said to what you interpreted, so I can communicate more effectively."

What you're communicating: "I need to know we're understanding instructions the same way. When I said [exact words], you thought that meant [wrong interpretation]. Can you explain how you got there? I'm trying to figure out how what I said became what you thought it meant, so I can explain better."

Breaking it down:

- **"I want to make sure we're interpreting instructions the same way"** = "I need to know you're understanding what I tell you"
- **"When I said [exact instruction], you understood that to mean [what they did]"** = "When I said [these specific words], you thought that meant [wrong thing]"
- **"Can you walk me through your thought process there?"** = "Can you explain how you got there?"
- **"I'm trying to understand how we got from what I said to what you interpreted"** = "I'm trying to figure out how my words became what you thought they meant"
- **"So I can communicate more effectively"** = "So I can explain things better"

More Direct: "There's a concerning pattern of misinterpretation I need to address. The instructions I provide are being understood in ways that don't align with what I actually said. When I said [specific instruction], that's direct and clear. What you delivered suggests you interpreted it as [their wrong interpretation], which isn't what those words mean. I need you to take instructions at face value without adding assumptions or reading between the lines that don't exist."

What you're communicating: "There's a worrying pattern where you keep misunderstanding me. You're understanding my instructions in ways that don't match what I actually said. When I said [specific words], that was direct and clear. What you did shows you thought it meant [wrong interpretation], which isn't what those words mean. You need to take instructions literally without adding assumptions or reading meanings that aren't there."

Breaking it down:

- **"There's a concerning pattern of misinterpretation I need to address"** = "There's a worrying pattern where you keep misunderstanding, and we need to fix it"
- **"The instructions I provide are being understood in ways that don't align with what I actually said"** = "You're understanding my instructions differently from what I actually said"
- **"When I said [specific instruction], that's direct and clear"** = "When I said [these words], that was straightforward"
- **"What you delivered suggests you interpreted it as [their wrong interpretation]"** = "What you did shows you thought it meant [wrong thing]"
- **"Which isn't what those words mean"** = "But that's not what those words mean"
- **"I need you to take instructions at face value"** = "You need to understand instructions literally"
- **"Without adding assumptions or reading between lines that don't exist"** = "Without adding your own guesses or finding hidden meanings that aren't there"

Firm: "We have a serious communication problem. You're consistently misinterpreting clear, direct instructions in ways that suggest you're either not reading carefully or you're adding your own interpretation where none is needed. When I give you an instruction, the words I use have specific meanings. I need you to follow what's actually said, not what you think might be implied. If something genuinely seems ambiguous, ask for clarification—but most of what I'm seeing isn't ambiguity. It's a misinterpretation of straightforward direction."

What you're communicating: "This is a major communication problem. You keep misunderstanding clear, simple instructions in ways that show you're either not reading carefully or you're making up your own meanings. When I give you instructions, the words I use mean specific things. You need to follow what I actually say, not what you guess might be hidden in there. If something truly seems unclear, ask me—but usually what I'm seeing isn't about unclear instructions. It's about you misunderstanding straightforward directions."

Breaking it down:

- **"We have a serious communication problem"** = "This is a major issue with how we communicate"
- **"You're consistently misinterpreting clear, direct instructions"** = "You keep misunderstanding simple, straightforward instructions"
- **"In ways that suggest you're either not reading carefully or you're adding your own interpretation where none is needed"** = "In ways that show you're either not reading carefully or making up meanings that aren't there"
- **"When I give you an instruction, the words I use have specific meanings"** = "The words I use mean specific things"
- **"I need you to follow what's actually said, not what you**

think might be implied" = "You need to do what I actually say, not what you think might be hidden"

- **"If something genuinely seems ambiguous, ask for clarification"** = "If something really seems unclear, ask me about it"
- **"But most of what I'm seeing isn't ambiguity. It's a misinterpretation of straightforward direction"** = "But usually the problem isn't unclear instructions. It's your misunderstanding of clear directions"

Why This Works: You're making it clear that this isn't about vague instructions—it's about them interpreting clear language incorrectly. By asking them to walk through their thought process, you're revealing where their thinking goes off track. The firm version draws the line: take instructions literally unless genuinely unclear, and ask for clarification rather than making assumptions.

Scenario 6: The Concept Just Isn't Clicking

Situation: You've explained a core concept that's fundamental to their role multiple ways—with examples, analogies, step-by-step breakdowns—and it's still not landing. Other people grasped it quickly. This person just can't seem to wrap their head around it, and it's limiting what they can do effectively.

What You're Thinking: "This is not a complicated concept. Everyone else understood this immediately. I've tried five different ways to explain it, and you're still looking at me like I'm speaking another language. Do you just not have the capacity to understand this? How can you do this job if you can't grasp this basic idea?"

What You Should Say:

Diplomatic: "I want to make sure you have a solid foundation in [concept]. We've approached it from a few different angles, and I'm sensing it still hasn't fully clicked. Sometimes concepts land better with different learning methods. Would it help to see it in action? Or to work through a practical example together? I want to find the approach that works for you, because understanding this concept is critical for your success in this role."

What you're communicating: "I need to make sure you really understand [concept]. We've tried explaining it in different ways, and I can tell you, you still don't fully get it. Sometimes people learn better with different methods. Would it help to watch someone do it? Or work through a real example together? I want to find a way that works for you, because you have to understand this to do your job well."

Breaking it down:

- **"I want to make sure you have a solid foundation in [concept]"** = "I need to know you really understand this important idea"
- **"We've approached it from a few different angles"** = "We've tried explaining it several different ways"
- **"And I'm sensing it still hasn't fully clicked"** = "And I can tell you still don't completely get it"
- **"Sometimes concepts land better with different learning methods"** = "Sometimes people understand better with different teaching approaches"
- **"Would it help to see it in action? Or to work through a practical example together?"** = "Would it help to watch it being done? Or practice with a real example?"
- **"I want to find the approach that works for you"** = "I want to find a way that helps you understand"

- **"Because understanding this concept is critical for your success in this role"** = "Because you must understand this to do your job well"

More Direct: "We need to address the ongoing difficulty with [concept]. This is a foundational element of your role, and despite multiple explanations and examples, it's not taking hold. At this point, I need you to take ownership of learning this—whether that means additional study time, seeking out other resources, or working with a peer who can explain it differently. This isn't optional knowledge—it's essential. The lack of comprehension here is limiting what you can do effectively."

What you're communicating: "We have to deal with the continuing problem of understanding [concept]. This is a basic part of your job, and even though I've explained it many times and given examples, you still don't get it. Now you need to take responsibility for learning this—maybe by studying more, finding other ways to learn it, or getting help from a coworker who can explain it differently. This isn't something you can skip—you have to know it. Not understanding this is preventing you from doing your job well."

Breaking it down:

- **"We need to address the ongoing difficulty with [concept]"** = "We have to deal with your continuing struggle to understand this idea"

- **"This is a foundational element of your role"** = "This is a basic, essential part of your job"

- **"And despite multiple explanations and examples, it's not taking hold"** = "And even after many explanations and examples, you still don't get it"

- **"At this point, I need you to take ownership of learning this"** = "Now you need to take responsibility for figuring this out"
- **"Whether that means additional study time, seeking out other resources, or working with a peer"** = "Maybe by studying more, finding other learning materials, or getting help from a coworker"
- **"Who can explain it differently"** = "Who might explain it in a way that works for you"
- **"This isn't optional knowledge—it's essential"** = "This isn't something nice to know—you must know it"
- **"The lack of comprehension here is limiting what you can do effectively"** = "Not understanding this is stopping you from doing your job well"

Firm: "I need to be direct: your inability to grasp [concept] has become a critical performance issue. This is fundamental knowledge for your position, and we've invested considerable time trying to help you understand it through multiple approaches. At this point, the gap isn't about how it's being taught—it's about whether you have the capacity to understand it at all. I need to see demonstrable understanding of this concept within [timeframe], or we need to have a serious conversation about your fit for this role. This is non-negotiable."

What you're communicating: "Let me be blunt: you not being able to understand [concept] is now a major problem with your job performance. This is basic knowledge you must have for your job, and we've spent a lot of time trying to help you understand it in many different ways. By now, the problem isn't about how we're teaching it—it's about whether you're even capable of understanding it. You need to show me you understand this within [timeframe], or we need to have a serious talk about whether you can do this job. You have to understand this—there's no way around it."

Breaking it down:

- **"I need to be direct: your inability to grasp [concept] has become a critical performance issue"** = "Let me be clear: you not being able to understand this is now a serious problem with your work"

- **"This is fundamental knowledge for your position"** = "This is basic knowledge your job requires"

- **"And we've invested considerable time trying to help you understand it through multiple approaches"** = "And we've spent a lot of time trying to teach you this many different ways"

- **"At this point, the gap isn't about how it's being taught—it's about whether you have the capacity to understand it at all"** = "By now, the problem isn't how we're explaining—it's whether you can even understand this"

- **"I need to see demonstrable understanding of this concept within [timeframe]"** = "You need to prove you understand this by [timeframe]"

- **"Or we need to have a serious conversation about your fit for this role"** = "Or we need to talk seriously about whether you belong in this job"

- **"This is non-negotiable"** = "This is required—there's no choice about it"

Why This Works: The diplomatic version offers one more attempt with a different learning approach while making it clear that this is critical. The direct version shifts responsibility to them to figure it out. The firm version makes it explicit that the inability to grasp fundamental concepts calls into question their capability for the role—it's no longer about teaching methods, it's about capacity.

HR-APPROVED PHRASE COLLECTION

Instead of "You're not getting this"

A. "I want to make sure we're aligned on [concept]."
B. "Let's revisit [concept] to ensure clarity."
C. "I'm seeing some confusion around [concept] that we need to address."
D. "It seems like there may be a gap in understanding about [concept]."
E. "Let me try explaining [concept] from a different angle."
F. "I want to ensure you have a solid grasp of [concept]."
G. "We need to build a stronger understanding of [concept]."
H. "This suggests we need to spend more time on [concept]."

Instead of "How many times do I have to explain this?"

A. "We've covered this a few times now—let's make sure it's sticking."
B. "I want to try a different approach since we're still seeing questions on this."
C. "We keep coming back to the same questions, which tells me we need to address the root confusion."
D. "I'm seeing repeated questions about things we've discussed multiple times."
E. "Let's find a way to make this information more accessible for you."
F. "We need to ensure this information is taking hold."

Instead of "You're solving for the wrong problem"

A. "I think we got our wires crossed on the objective here."

B. "Let's make sure we're aligned on what problem we're actually solving."
C. "This addresses [X], but what we need is [Y]."
D. "There's a disconnect between the ask and the deliverable."
E. "Let's back up and clarify the core issue we're trying to address."
F. "I need to ensure you understand the fundamental goal of this work."

Instead of "You're missing obvious connections"

A. "Let's talk about how we're thinking through cause and effect here."
B. "I want to help you build the skill of anticipating consequences."
C. "We need to work on connecting actions to their likely outcomes."
D. "I'm seeing gaps in how we're thinking through the chain of events."
E. "This outcome was fairly predictable based on [X]—let's discuss why."
F. "We need to strengthen analytical thinking around [concept]."

Instead of "Are you even listening?"

A. "I want to make sure information is landing when we talk."
B. "Let's ensure we're capturing key points from our conversations."
C. "I'm noticing questions about things we've already covered."
D. "I need you to take notes during our discussions so nothing gets missed."
E. "When we talk about important items, I need your full attention."
F. "We need to find a way to make sure information sticks from our conversations."

Instead of "You're twisting what I said"

A. "I want to make sure we're interpreting instructions the same way."
B. "Let's clarify what I meant versus how it was understood."
C. "I'm seeing a pattern where instructions are being interpreted differently than intended."
D. "When I say [X], I mean [X]—not [Y]."
E. "I need you to take instructions at face value without adding assumptions."
F. "If something seems ambiguous, please ask rather than interpreting."

Instead of "This is simple and you're making it complicated"

A. "I think we might be overthinking this concept."
B. "Let's break this down to its most basic elements."
C. "This is more straightforward than it might seem."
D. "I want to simplify this for clarity."
E. "We're adding complexity where it doesn't need to exist."
F. "Let's focus on the core principle without the extra layers."

Instead of "Everyone else understood this immediately"

A. "This concept typically clicks quickly for people in this role."
B. "Most team members grasp this after one or two explanations."
C. "This is generally considered foundational knowledge for this position."
D. "Other people haven't struggled with this concept to the same degree."
E. "This is standard understanding for someone at your level."

Instead of "You lack critical thinking skills"

A. "We need to strengthen analytical reasoning skills."
B. "I need to see more evidence of strategic thinking."
C. "This role requires strong problem-solving capabilities."
D. "We need to develop your ability to think through complex scenarios."
E. "I'm looking for more critical analysis in your approach."
F. "The level of reasoning demonstrated here needs improvement."

Instead of "You're not smart enough for this"

A. "This role requires capabilities we need to develop further."
B. "There's a gap between the cognitive demands of this position and the current skill level."
C. "We need to assess whether this role is the right fit for your strengths."
D. "The complexity of this work may not align with your current capacity."
E. "This position requires analytical abilities that need significant development."

When repeated explanations aren't working

A. "Despite multiple approaches, this concept isn't taking hold."
B. "We've tried several ways to explain this, and it's still not clicking."
C. "I've explained this from multiple angles without success."
D. "We need to find a different strategy because current approaches aren't working."
E. "At this point, the issue isn't how I'm explaining—it's about finding what works for you."

For pattern recognition issues

A. "I'm seeing difficulty recognizing patterns in [area]."
B. "You're not connecting dots that should be fairly obvious."
C. "There's a gap in seeing how these elements relate to each other."
D. "We need to work on identifying relationships between [X] and [Y]."
E. "The ability to spot patterns is critical for this work."

When they think they understand, but don't

A. "I need to verify understanding rather than assume it."
B. "Let's test comprehension by having you explain this back to me."
C. "Your work suggests a different understanding than what you expressed."
D. "There's a gap between stated comprehension and demonstrated understanding."
E. "I need to see evidence that this concept has actually landed."

For misunderstanding the objectives

A. "We need to align on the 'why' behind this work."
B. "Let's ensure we understand the business objective, not just the task."
C. "I need you to articulate back what we're trying to accomplish and why."
D. "There's confusion about the fundamental goal here."
E. "We're not aligned on what success looks like for this project."

When instructions are consistently misinterpreted

A. "Instructions are being understood in ways that don't match what was communicated."
B. "We have a pattern of misalignment between what's said and what's heard."
C. "I need you to confirm understanding before beginning work."
D. "When I provide direction, please repeat back what you heard to ensure alignment."
E. "We need to close the gap between instruction and interpretation."

Chapter 3 Quick Reference Box

Ten Essential Phrases for Comprehension Issues

1. "We've covered this multiple times—let's identify where the disconnect is so we can move forward."

2. "Walk me through your understanding of [concept] so I can see where we need to clarify."

3. "This addresses [X], but what we actually need is [Y]. Let's ensure we're aligned on the objective."

4. "I'm seeing questions about things we discussed in the same conversation—I need your full attention during important discussions."

5. "When I said [X], you interpreted it as [Y]. Let's clarify: I meant [X] literally, without additional assumptions."

6. "Let's work on connecting actions to consequences—anticipating what's likely to happen as a result of certain decisions."

7. "Despite multiple approaches, this concept isn't taking hold. I need you to take ownership of learning this through additional study or resources."

8. "There's a pattern of misinterpretation I need to address. Instructions need to be taken at face value unless genuinely ambiguous."

9. "This is foundational knowledge for your role. The ongoing difficulty grasping it has become a performance concern."

10. "I need to see demonstrable understanding of [concept] within [timeframe], or we need to discuss whether this role aligns with your capabilities."

FOUR
MISSED DEADLINES & POOR TIME MANAGEMENT

"I Need You to Prioritize Better"
(Translation: Stop Wasting Time)

Real Talk

There's a special frustration reserved for the employee who treats deadlines like vague suggestions rather than actual commitments. You set a due date three weeks out—plenty of time for the work required. And then, the day before it's due, you get the email: "I'm going to need more time on this." Or worse, the deadline passes with radio silence, and when you follow up, they seem genuinely surprised that you expected it to be done.

Maybe they're terrible at estimating how long things take. Maybe they procrastinate until panic sets in. Maybe they're working on the wrong things entirely and don't realize the clock is ticking. Or maybe they just don't feel the same urgency you do when a deadline approaches, treating it as negotiable rather than fixed.

The pattern becomes clear: deadlines arrive, and they're not ready. There's always a reason—they underestimated the complexity, something unexpected came up, they needed to perfect it—but the excuses don't change the impact. Projects fall behind. Other people's work gets delayed. You're stuck explaining to your own boss why commitments aren't being met. And you're left managing someone who apparently needs a countdown timer and daily reminders to take deadlines seriously.

You can't say "do you not understand what a deadline means?" or "everyone else manages to finish on time" or "I'm tired of your excuses." But you also can't let someone operate in their own timezone while the rest of the team is held to actual schedules. This chapter gives you the language to address deadline and time management issues without sounding unreasonable or creating claims of excessive pressure.

Five Principles for the Time Management Conversation

- **Distinguish between one-time misses and patterns.** Everyone occasionally needs an extension. Chronic deadline issues are a different conversation.

- **Connect deadlines to downstream impact.** Help them understand that their timeline affects other people, projects, and business outcomes—it's not arbitrary.

- **Require early flags, not last-minute notifications.** If they can't meet a deadline, you need to know with enough time to adjust plans, not the day before.

- **Address both the symptom and the cause.** Missing deadlines is the visible problem. Poor planning, underestimation, or misplaced priorities might be the real issue.

- **Set clear expectations going forward.** Don't assume they'll magically improve. Establish specific standards for what "on time" means and what you need from them.

Let's Get Real Scenarios

Scenario 1: "I Thought I Had More Time" (The Deadline Was Three Weeks Ago)

Situation: An employee misses a deadline that was clearly communicated well in advance. When you follow up, they express surprise or claim they didn't realize how soon it was due—despite multiple reminders and the fact that it's been on the calendar for weeks. This isn't a matter of unexpected obstacles; it's a matter of not paying attention to timelines.

What You're Thinking: "The deadline was literally on the calendar for a month. I mentioned it in three separate meetings. How are you surprised? Did you think time would magically stop? Were you planning to start working on it the day it was due?"

What You Should Say:

Diplomatic: "I want to talk about the timeline for [project]. The deadline was [date], and I'm not seeing it completed. Help me understand what happened—were there obstacles that prevented progress, or was there confusion about when this was due? Going forward, I need you to flag potential deadline issues well in advance so we can address them before they become problems."

What you're communicating: "We need to discuss why this wasn't done when it was supposed to be finished on [date]. Tell me what went wrong—did something block you, or did you not realize when it was due? From now on, if you're going to miss a deadline, you need to tell me way ahead of time so we can fix it before it becomes a crisis."

Breaking it down:

- **"I want to talk about the timeline for [project]"** = "We need to discuss why this is late"
- **"The deadline was [date], and I'm not seeing it completed"** = "This was supposed to be done on [date], and it's not"

- **"Help me understand what happened"** = "Explain to me what went wrong"
- **"Were there obstacles that prevented progress, or was there confusion about when this was due?"** = "Did something block you, or did you just not know when it was due?"
- **"Going forward, I need you to flag potential deadline issues well in advance"** = "From now on, tell me early if you're going to be late"
- **"So we can address them before they become problems"** = "So we can fix things before it's a crisis"

More Direct: "We have a missed deadline that we need to address. This was due on [date], with multiple reminders leading up to it. The fact that it's not complete tells me either you weren't tracking the timeline appropriately or you weren't prioritizing this work. I need to understand which one it is, because both are issues we need to fix. Deadlines aren't flexible unless we discuss it in advance."

What you're communicating: "You missed a deadline, and we need to talk about it. This was supposed to be done on [date], and I reminded you several times. The fact that it's not finished means either you weren't keeping track of when it was due or you weren't making this a priority. I need to know which one, because both are problems. You can't just change deadlines without talking to me first."

Breaking it down:

- **"We have a missed deadline that we need to address"** = "You missed a deadline and we need to talk about it"
- **"This was due on [date], with multiple reminders leading up to it"** = "This was supposed to be done on [date], and I reminded you many times"

- **"The fact that it's not complete tells me either you weren't tracking the timeline appropriately"** = "Since it's not done, either you weren't keeping track of the deadline"
- **"Or you weren't prioritizing this work"** = "Or you weren't making this important enough"
- **"I need to understand which one it is, because both are issues we need to fix"** = "Tell me which one, because both are problems we have to solve"
- **"Deadlines aren't flexible unless we discuss it in advance"** = "You can't just change deadlines without talking to me first"

Firm: "We need to have a serious conversation about this missed deadline. This was due on [date]—that wasn't a suggestion or a rough target. That was a commitment that you failed to meet without advance notice. This affects project timelines, team coordination, and my ability to deliver on our commitments. I need you to understand that deadlines are firm unless we have a conversation before they arrive. This kind of mistake can't happen again."

What you're communicating: "We need to have a serious talk about you missing this deadline. This was supposed to be done on [date]—that wasn't a maybe or an estimate. That was a real deadline that you didn't meet and didn't warn me about. This messes up the whole project schedule, makes it harder for the team to coordinate, and makes it so I can't keep the promises I made. You need to understand that deadlines are real and fixed unless we talk about changing them beforehand. You can't miss deadlines like this again."

Breaking it down:

- **"We need to have a serious conversation about this missed deadline"** = "We need to have a serious talk about you missing this deadline"

- **"This was due on [date]—that wasn't a suggestion or a rough target"** = "This was supposed to be done on [date]—that wasn't flexible or approximate"

- **"That was a commitment that you failed to meet without advance notice"** = "That was a real deadline you didn't meet and didn't warn me about"

- **"This affects project timelines, team coordination, and my ability to deliver on our commitments"** = "This messes up the project schedule, the team's work, and my ability to keep promises"

- **"I need you to understand that deadlines are firm unless we have a conversation before they arrive"** = "You need to know deadlines are real unless we talk about changing them beforehand"

- **"This kind of miss can't happen again"** = "You can't miss deadlines like this again"

Why This Works: You're making it clear that the deadline wasn't ambiguous or negotiable. By asking what happened, you're giving them a chance to explain while making it obvious you expected better. The firm version establishes consequences and makes explicit that deadlines are commitments, not suggestions.

Scenario 2: Last-Minute Panic That Could Have Been Avoided

Situation: An employee comes to you in a panic right before something is due, suddenly realizing they can't finish on time. The deadline has been known for weeks. The work required was clear. But they waited until the last minute to assess progress, and now there's a crisis that could have been avoided with basic planning.

What You're Thinking: "You've known about this deadline for three weeks. Why are you just now realizing you're not going to make it? Where was the panic two weeks ago when you could have done something about it? Did you think it would somehow work itself out?"

What You Should Say:

Diplomatic: "I appreciate you letting me know you're behind, but I'm concerned this is coming up so close to the deadline. This project has been on your plate for [timeframe], and ideally, I would have known about timeline concerns earlier. Let's talk about how you're tracking progress on projects so we can catch these issues before they become last-minute crises. What would help you assess whether you're on track before the deadline arrives?"

What you're communicating: "I'm glad you told me you're behind, but I'm worried you're only telling me now when the deadline is so close. You've had this project for [timeframe], and I should have known about the problems much earlier. Let's figure out how you're keeping track of your work so we can find these issues before they become emergencies. What would help you figure out if you're on schedule before it's too late?"

Breaking it down:

- **"I appreciate you letting me know you're behind"** = "I'm glad you told me there's a problem"
- **"But I'm concerned this is coming up so close to the deadline"** = "But I'm worried you're only telling me now when the deadline is almost here"
- **"This project has been on your plate for [timeframe]"** = "You've had this work for [timeframe]"
- **"And ideally I would have known about timeline concerns earlier"** = "And I should have known about problems much sooner"

- **"Let's talk about how you're tracking progress on projects"** = "Let's discuss how you're keeping track of your work"
- **"So we can catch these issues before they become last-minute crises"** = "So we can find problems before they become emergencies"
- **"What would help you assess whether you're on track before the deadline arrives?"** = "What would help you know if you're on schedule before it's too late?"

More Direct: "The issue isn't just that you're running behind—it's that I'm finding out about it now, when there's no time to adjust. You've had [timeframe] to work on this, which means you should have identified this problem days or weeks ago. I need you to build in progress checks so you're flagging timeline issues early, not when it's too late to do anything about them. Last-minute emergencies that could have been prevented aren't acceptable."

What you're communicating: "The problem isn't only that you're late—it's that you're telling me now when it's too late to fix anything. You've had [timeframe] to do this work, so you should have seen this problem days or weeks ago. You need to check your progress regularly so you can tell me about timeline problems early, not when there's no time left. Creating emergencies that could have been avoided isn't okay."

Breaking it down:

- **"The issue isn't just that you're running behind"** = "The problem isn't only that you're late"
- **"It's that I'm finding out about it now, when there's no time to adjust"** = "It's that you're telling me now when it's too late to fix anything"

- **"You've had [timeframe] to work on this"** = "You've had [timeframe] for this work"
- **"Which means you should have identified this problem days or weeks ago"** = "So you should have seen this problem much earlier"
- **"I need you to build in progress checks"** = "You need to check how you're doing regularly"
- **"So you're flagging timeline issues early, not when it's too late to do anything about them"** = "So you tell me about problems early, not when there's no time left"
- **"Last-minute emergencies that could have been prevented aren't acceptable"** = "Creating crises that didn't need to happen isn't okay"

Firm: "This is exactly the kind of situation I need to avoid. You're coming to me the day before the deadline to tell me you can't finish—but you've had [timeframe] to work on this. That tells me you're not monitoring your own progress or planning your work effectively. This creates unnecessary pressure on everyone and limits our options to address the problem. Going forward, I expect you to check in on your progress regularly and flag concerns at least [X days] before a deadline. This pattern of last-minute revelations has to stop."

What you're communicating: "This is exactly what I need to prevent. You're telling me the day before it's due that you can't finish—but you've had [timeframe] to do this. That shows me you're not checking your own progress or planning your work well. This creates stress for everyone and makes it so we can't really fix the problem. From now on, you need to check how you're doing regularly and tell me about problems at least [X days] before things are due. You can't keep surprising me at the last minute like this."

Breaking it down:

- **"This is exactly the kind of situation I need to avoid"** = "This is precisely what I need to prevent"
- **"You're coming to me the day before the deadline to tell me you can't finish"** = "You're telling me the day before it's due that you won't be done"
- **"But you've had [timeframe] to work on this"** = "But you've had [timeframe] to do this work"
- **"That tells me you're not monitoring your own progress or planning your work effectively"** = "That shows me you're not checking how you're doing or planning well"
- **"This creates unnecessary pressure on everyone and limits our options to address the problem"** = "This causes stress for everyone and makes it so we can't really fix things"
- **"Going forward, I expect you to check in on your progress regularly"** = "From now on, you need to check your progress often"
- **"And flag concerns at least [X days] before a deadline"** = "And tell me about problems at least [X days] before things are due"
- **"This pattern of last-minute revelations has to stop"** = "You have to stop surprising me at the last minute"

Why This Works: You're addressing both the missed deadline and the late notification. By asking about their progress tracking, you're surfacing the root cause—they're not monitoring their own work. The firm version makes it clear that last-minute surprises are unacceptable and sets specific expectations for early warning.

Scenario 3: "I'm Working on It" Has Lost All Meaning

Situation: Every time you check in on a project, the employee says they're "working on it" or "making progress," but when the deadline arrives, the work is either incomplete or barely started. The vague assurances masked a lack of actual progress, and you're left with an unfinished project and no clear sense of where the time went.

What You're Thinking: "You've been 'working on it' for two weeks and this is what I get? What does 'working on it' even mean to you? Five minutes of effort spread over ten days? You clearly weren't working on it enough, because it's nowhere near done."

What You Should Say:

Diplomatic: "I want to make sure we're on the same page about progress. When I've checked in, you've indicated you're working on this, but now that we're at the deadline, I'm seeing it's not complete. Help me understand where the gap is—what does 'working on it' look like in terms of actual time invested and tasks completed? Going forward, I need more specific updates than 'working on it'—I need to know what's been done and what's left."

What you're communicating: "I need to make sure we both understand what 'making progress' means. When I've asked about this, you've said you're working on it, but now that it's due, it's not finished. Help me understand the disconnect—when you say you're 'working on it,' how much time are you actually spending, and what tasks are you actually finishing? From now on, I need detailed updates, not just 'working on it'—I need to know what you've actually done and what still needs to be done."

Breaking it down:

- **"I want to make sure we're on the same page about progress"** = "I need to make sure we both understand what progress means"

- **"When I've checked in, you've indicated you're working on this"** = "When I've asked, you've said you're working on it"
- **"But now that we're at the deadline, I'm seeing it's not complete"** = "But now that it's due, it's not finished"
- **"Help me understand where the gap is"** = "Help me understand the disconnect"
- **"What does 'working on it' look like in terms of actual time invested and tasks completed?"** = "When you say 'working on it,' how much time are you really spending and what are you actually finishing?"
- **"Going forward, I need more specific updates than 'working on it'"** = "From now on, I need detailed updates, not vague ones"
- **"I need to know what's been done and what's left"** = "I need to know what you've finished and what still needs to be done"

More Direct: "There's a disconnect between your progress updates and the actual state of this work. Each time I've checked in, you've told me you're working on it, but the deliverable doesn't reflect meaningful progress. I need you to be more accurate when assessing your status. 'Working on it' isn't helpful if the work isn't moving forward. From now on, I need you to tell me specifically what you've completed, not just that you're working on it. And if you're stuck or behind, I need to know that, not hear vague assurances."

What you're communicating: "What you've been telling me about your progress doesn't match the actual status of the work. Every time I've asked, you've said you're working on it, but the work itself doesn't show real progress. You need to be more honest about where you actually are. Saying 'working on it' doesn't help if the work isn't actually moving forward. From now on, tell me exactly what you've finished, not just that you're working on it. And if you're stuck or behind schedule, tell me that truth, not vague reassurances."

Breaking it down:

- **"There's a disconnect between your progress updates and the actual state of this work"** = "What you tell me about progress doesn't match how the work actually looks"
- **"Each time I've checked in, you've told me you're working on it"** = "Every time I've asked, you've said you're working on it"
- **"But the deliverable doesn't reflect meaningful progress"** = "But the work doesn't show real progress"
- **"I need you to be more accurate when assessing your status"** = "You need to be more honest about where you actually are"
- **"'Working on it' isn't helpful if the work isn't moving forward"** = "Saying 'working on it' doesn't help if nothing is actually getting done"
- **"From now on, I need you to tell me specifically what you've completed"** = "From now on, tell me exactly what you've finished"
- **"Not just that you're working on it"** = "Not just vague statements about working on it"
- **"And if you're stuck or behind, I need to know that, not hear vague assurances"** = "And if you're stuck or late, tell me that truth, not vague reassurances"

Firm: "We have a serious problem. You've consistently told me you're working on this project, but the actual progress doesn't support that claim. Either you're significantly overestimating your progress or you're not being transparent about where things actually stand. Both are issues. I need complete honesty about project status going forward. If you're on track, tell me what's complete. If you're behind, I need to know immediately—not at the deadline. Misleading progress updates waste everyone's time and prevent us from addressing problems while we still can."

What you're communicating: "This is a serious problem. You've kept telling me you're working on this, but the actual progress doesn't prove that. Either you're totally misjudging how much you've actually done, or you're not being honest about where things really are. Both are problems. From now on, I need complete honesty about where projects really stand. If you're on schedule, tell me what you've actually finished. If you're behind, tell me right away—not when it's due. Giving me false updates wastes everyone's time and stops us from fixing problems when we still have time."

Breaking it down:

- **"We have a serious problem"** = "This is a serious issue"
- **"You've consistently told me you're working on this project"** = "You've kept telling me you're working on this"
- **"But the actual progress doesn't support that claim"** = "But the real progress doesn't prove that"
- **"Either you're significantly overestimating your progress"** = "Either you're totally misjudging how much you've done"
- **"Or you're not being transparent about where things actually stand"** = "Or you're not being honest about where things really are"
- **"Both are issues"** = "Both are problems"

- **"I need complete honesty about project status going forward"** = "From now on, I need total honesty about where projects stand"

- **"If you're on track, tell me what's complete. If you're behind, I need to know immediately—not at the deadline"** = "If you're on schedule, tell me what's done. If you're late, tell me right away—not when it's due"

- **"Misleading progress updates waste everyone's time and prevent us from addressing problems while we still can"** = "False updates waste everyone's time and stop us from fixing problems when we can"

Why This Works: You're calling out the gap between what they said and what actually exists. By asking for specific progress details going forward, you're eliminating the ability to hide behind vague assurances. The firm version makes it clear that misleading updates are as much of a problem as the missed deadline itself.

Scenario 4: The Person Who Underestimates Every Task

Situation: This employee consistently underestimates how long tasks will take. They commit to tight timelines with confidence, and then inevitably can't deliver. Whether it's optimism or poor judgment, their estimates are consistently wrong, and it's affecting planning for the entire team.

What You're Thinking: "You said this would take two days. It's been a week, and you're not even halfway done. How are you this bad at estimating your own work? Do you just say whatever sounds good without actually thinking about what's involved? This happens every single time."

What You Should Say:

Diplomatic: "I want to talk about timeline estimation. I'm noticing that projects consistently take longer than you initially estimate. For example, [specific instance]. This makes it difficult to plan effectively. Let's work on building more accurate estimates—that might mean adding buffer time, breaking work into smaller pieces to estimate better, or checking with me before committing to timelines. What do you think would help you estimate more realistically?"

What you're communicating: "We need to discuss how you estimate how long things will take. Your estimates keep being wrong—projects take much longer than you say they will, like, [specific example]. This makes it hard to plan. Let's figure out how you can estimate more accurately—maybe you need to add extra time, break work into smaller parts to estimate better, or check with me before promising deadlines. What would help you estimate more realistically?"

Breaking it down:

- **"I want to talk about timeline estimation"** = "We need to discuss how you predict how long work will take"
- **"I'm noticing that projects consistently take longer than you initially estimate"** = "Projects keep taking longer than you say they will"
- **"For example, [specific instance]"** = "Like [specific example]"
- **"This makes it difficult to plan effectively"** = "This makes it hard to plan properly"
- **"Let's work on building more accurate estimates"** = "Let's figure out how to make better predictions"
- **"That might mean adding buffer time, breaking work into smaller pieces to estimate better, or checking with me before committing to timelines"** = "Maybe you need to add extra

time, split work into smaller tasks to estimate better, or ask me before promising deadlines"

- **"What do you think would help you estimate more realistically?"** = "What would help you predict timeframes more accurately?"

More Direct: "We need to address a pattern with your timeline commitments. You consistently underestimate how long work will take, and then can't deliver on the timelines you've set. This isn't a one-time issue—it's happening repeatedly. This affects project planning, team coordination, and my ability to set accurate expectations with stakeholders. Going forward, I need you to either improve your estimation skills or build in significant buffer time. When you commit to a timeline, I need confidence it's achievable."

What you're communicating: "We need to fix a problem with the deadlines you promise. You keep underestimating how long work takes, and then you can't meet the deadlines you set. This isn't just happening once—it keeps happening. This messes up project planning, team coordination, and my ability to give accurate timelines to others. From now on, you need to either get better at estimating or add a lot of extra time to your estimates. When you promise a deadline, I need to know you can actually meet it."

Breaking it down:

- **"We need to address a pattern with your timeline commitments"** = "We need to fix a problem with the deadlines you promise"
- **"You consistently underestimate how long work will take"** = "You keep predicting work will take less time than it actually does"

- **"And then can't deliver on the timelines you've set"** = "And then you can't meet the deadlines you promised"
- **"This isn't a one-time issue—it's happening repeatedly"** = "This isn't just once—it keeps happening"
- **"This affects project planning, team coordination, and my ability to set accurate expectations with stakeholders"** = "This messes up planning, the team's work, and my ability to give accurate timelines to others"
- **"Going forward, I need you to either improve your estimation skills or build in significant buffer time"** = "From now on, you need to get better at estimating or add lots of extra time"
- **"When you commit to a timeline, I need confidence it's achievable"** = "When you promise a deadline, I need to know you can meet it"

Firm: "I need to be direct: your inability to accurately estimate work is creating serious problems. You commit to timelines with confidence, and then consistently fail to deliver. This isn't about unexpected obstacles—this is about fundamentally misjudging how long your own work takes. I can't rely on your estimates, which means I can't plan effectively or make commitments based on your timelines. Going forward, all deadline commitments need to go through me first. I need to see demonstrated improvement in your ability to assess work accurately, or you won't be setting your own timelines."

What you're communicating: "Let me be blunt: you're really bad at estimating how long work takes, and it's causing major problems. You promise deadlines confidently, and then you keep failing to meet them. This isn't about unexpected problems—this is about being completely wrong about how long your own work takes. I can't trust your estimates anymore, which means I can't plan properly or make promises based on your timelines. From now on, you have to check with me before promising any deadline. You need to get much better at judging how long work takes, or you won't be allowed to set your own deadlines anymore."

Breaking it down:

- **"I need to be direct: your inability to accurately estimate work is creating serious problems"** = "Let me be blunt: you're bad at estimating and it's causing big problems"
- **"You commit to timelines with confidence, and then consistently fail to deliver"** = "You promise deadlines confidently, then you keep missing them"
- **"This isn't about unexpected obstacles—this is about fundamentally misjudging how long your own work takes"** = "This isn't about surprises—this is about being wrong about how long your work takes"
- **"I can't rely on your estimates, which means I can't plan effectively or make commitments based on your timelines"** = "I can't trust your predictions, so I can't plan well or make promises based on your deadlines"
- **"Going forward, all deadline commitments need to go through me first"** = "From now on, you have to check with me before promising any deadline"
- **"I need to see demonstrated improvement in your ability to assess work accurately"** = "You need to get much better at judging how long work takes"
- **"Or you won't be setting your own timelines"** = "Or you won't be allowed to set deadlines anymore"

Why This Works: You're identifying the specific pattern—chronic underestimation—without saying they're incompetent. By offering solutions (buffer time, checking with you first), you're giving them a path forward. The firm version establishes that if they can't estimate accurately, they lose the autonomy to set their own deadlines.

Scenario 5: Excuses Are Constant, But Results Are Absent

Situation: Every missed deadline comes with an explanation. There's always something that gets in the way—other priorities, unclear requirements, technical issues, personal matters. The excuses might even be legitimate individually, but the pattern is clear: something always prevents them from delivering on time, and at a certain point, the reasons stop mattering.

What You're Thinking: "There's always something, isn't there? I'm not saying these things didn't happen, but somehow they only happen to you, and somehow they always happen right before your deadlines. At what point do you take responsibility for managing around obstacles like everyone else does?"

What You Should Say:

Diplomatic: "I understand that obstacles come up—they do for everyone. What concerns me is the pattern where each deadline we've discussed has come with a reason it couldn't be met. [Technical issue], [other priority], [personal matter]—individually, these are understandable, but collectively, they suggest we need to either build in more buffer time, improve at identifying issues earlier, or find ways to work around obstacles that arise. Let's talk about how to prevent this pattern from continuing."

What you're communicating: "I know that problems happen to everyone. What worries me is that every single deadline you've had has come with an excuse for why you couldn't meet it. [Technical problem], [other work], [personal issue]—any one of these makes sense, but when they all keep happening, it shows we need to either give you more time, get better at spotting problems sooner, or figure out how to work around issues when they come up. Let's talk about how to stop this pattern."

Breaking it down:

- **"I understand that obstacles come up—they do for everyone"** = "I know problems happen to everyone"
- **"What concerns me is the pattern where each deadline we've discussed has come with a reason it couldn't be met"** = "What worries me is that every deadline has come with an excuse"
- **"[Technical issue], [other priority], [personal matter]—individually these are understandable"** = "Any one reason makes sense on its own"
- **"But collectively they suggest we need to either build in more buffer time, improve at identifying issues earlier, or find ways to work around obstacles"** = "But all together they show we need to give more time, spot problems sooner, or work around issues better"
- **"Let's talk about how to prevent this pattern from continuing"** = "Let's discuss how to stop this from happening"

More Direct: "I want to address something I'm seeing: there's always a reason why deadlines can't be met. I'm not questioning the legitimacy of individual obstacles, but the pattern concerns me. Everyone faces unexpected issues, but most people find ways to deliver on time despite them. I need you to take more ownership of managing around obstacles rather than treating them as reasons deadlines don't apply. If something is genuinely going to prevent you from meeting a deadline, I need advance notice—not an explanation after the fact."

What you're communicating: "I need to talk about something: there's always a reason why you can't meet deadlines. I'm not saying each excuse is fake, but the pattern worries me. Everyone deals with unexpected problems, but most people still finish on time anyway. You need to take more responsibility for working around obstacles instead of using them as reasons why deadlines don't count. If something is really going to make you late, tell me ahead of time—don't explain after you've already missed it."

Breaking it down:

- **"I want to address something I'm seeing: there's always a reason why deadlines can't be met"** = "I need to talk about a pattern: there's always an excuse for missing deadlines"
- **"I'm not questioning the legitimacy of individual obstacles"** = "I'm not saying each excuse is fake"
- **"But the pattern concerns me"** = "But the constant pattern worries me"
- **"Everyone faces unexpected issues, but most people find ways to deliver on time despite them"** = "Everyone has surprise problems, but most people still finish on time anyway"
- **"I need you to take more ownership of managing around obstacles"** = "You need to take more responsibility for working around problems"
- **"Rather than treating them as reasons deadlines don't apply"** = "Instead of using them as reasons why deadlines don't matter"
- **"If something is genuinely going to prevent you from meeting a deadline, I need advance notice—not an explanation after the fact"** = "If something will really make

you late, tell me ahead of time—don't explain after you've missed it"

Firm: "We need to have a frank conversation. Every single deadline we've discussed has come with a reason it couldn't be met. At this point, the specific reasons matter less than the pattern of non-delivery. Other team members face similar obstacles and still meet deadlines. The difference is they plan for contingencies, flag issues early, and find ways to deliver despite challenges. I need to see that same level of accountability from you. Going forward, I'm not interested in reasons after deadlines pass—I need proactive communication before they're missed and actual delivery when you commit to a timeline."

What you're communicating: "We need to have an honest talk. Every single deadline has come with an excuse for why you couldn't meet it. At this point, the specific reasons don't matter as much as the pattern of not finishing. Other people deal with similar problems and still finish on time. The difference is they plan for backup options, warn people early about issues, and figure out how to finish anyway. I need to see that same responsibility from you. From now on, I don't want to hear reasons after you've already missed deadlines—I need you to tell me ahead of time if there's a problem, and I need you to actually deliver when you promise something."

Breaking it down:

- **"We need to have a frank conversation"** = "We need to have an honest talk"

- **"Every single deadline we've discussed has come with a reason it couldn't be met"** = "Every deadline has come with an excuse for why you couldn't meet it"

- **"At this point, the specific reasons matter less than the pattern of non-delivery"** = "Now, the actual reasons matter less than the pattern of not finishing"

- **"Other team members face similar obstacles and still meet deadlines"** = "Other people have similar problems and still finish on time"
- **"The difference is they plan for contingencies, flag issues early, and find ways to deliver despite challenges"** = "The difference is they plan for problems, warn people early, and figure out how to finish anyway"
- **"I need to see that same level of accountability from you"** = "I need to see that same responsibility from you"
- **"Going forward, I'm not interested in reasons after deadlines pass"** = "From now on, I don't want reasons after you've missed deadlines"
- **"I need proactive communication before they're missed and actual delivery when you commit to a timeline"** = "I need you to tell me ahead of time if there's a problem, and actually finish when you promise"

Why This Works: You're acknowledging that individual obstacles are real while making it clear the pattern is unacceptable. By pointing out that others face similar challenges and still deliver, you're establishing that obstacles don't excuse missed deadlines. The firm version draws the line: no more post-deadline explanations without pre-deadline warnings and better results.

Scenario 6: They're Surprised by Predictable Deadlines

Situation: Despite clear advance notice, the employee seems genuinely surprised when deadlines arrive. They act as if the due date snuck up on them, even though it was on the calendar, mentioned in meetings, and clearly communicated from the start. The deadline didn't change —but they apparently forgot it existed.

What You're Thinking: "How are you surprised? This has been on the calendar for a month. It's been in every status meeting. I sent three reminder emails. Did you think it was decorative? At what point were you planning to actually start working on this?"

What You Should Say:

Diplomatic: "I want to make sure we have a system for tracking deadlines. When [project] came due, it seemed like the timeline was a surprise, even though we'd discussed it multiple times and it was on the calendar. Help me understand how you're tracking your commitments—what tools or processes are you using to stay on top of due dates? We need to find a system that works so deadlines aren't catching you off guard."

What you're communicating: "I need to make sure you have a way to keep track of deadlines. When [project] was due, it seemed like you didn't know it was coming, even though we'd talked about it many times and it was on the calendar. Tell me how you're keeping track of your work—what are you using to remember when things are due? We need to find something that works so you don't get surprised by deadlines."

Breaking it down:

- **"I want to make sure we have a system for tracking deadlines"** = "I need to know you have a way to track when things are due"
- **"When [project] came due, it seemed like the timeline was a surprise"** = "When [project] was due, you seemed shocked"
- **"Even though we'd discussed it multiple times and it was on the calendar"** = "Even though we'd talked about it many times and it was written down"
- **"Help me understand how you're tracking your**

commitments" = "Explain to me how you remember what you need to do"

- **"What tools or processes are you using to stay on top of due dates?"** = "What are you using to keep track of deadlines?"
- **"We need to find a system that works so deadlines aren't catching you off guard"** = "We need something that works so you're not surprised by due dates"

More Direct: "I'm concerned about how you're managing deadlines. This due date was communicated [timeframe] in advance, mentioned in [number] meetings, and documented in [location]. Despite all of that, it appears to have caught you off guard. That tells me you're not tracking your work commitments effectively. Going forward, you need to take ownership of deadline awareness—that means maintaining a system that works for you, setting your own reminders, and proactively checking your calendar. I shouldn't have to remind you about deadlines that were clearly established."

What you're communicating: "I'm worried about how you handle deadlines. This due date was announced [timeframe] ahead of time, mentioned in [number] meetings, and written in [location]. Even with all that, you seemed surprised when it arrived. This shows me you're not keeping track of your work properly. From now on, you need to take responsibility for knowing when things are due—that means having a system that works for you, setting your own alerts, and checking your calendar regularly. I shouldn't have to keep reminding you about deadlines that were already clearly set."

Breaking it down:

- **"I'm concerned about how you're managing deadlines"** = "I'm worried about how you handle due dates"

- **"This due date was communicated [timeframe] in advance, mentioned in [number] meetings, and documented in [location]"** = "This deadline was announced early, talked about multiple times, and written down"

- **"Despite all of that, it appears to have caught you off guard"** = "Even with all that, you seemed surprised"

- **"That tells me you're not tracking your work commitments effectively"** = "This shows me you're not keeping track of your work well"

- **"Going forward, you need to take ownership of deadline awareness"** = "From now on, you need to be responsible for knowing when things are due"

- **"That means maintaining a system that works for you, setting your own reminders, and proactively checking your calendar"** = "That means having a system, setting alerts, and checking your calendar yourself"

- **"I shouldn't have to remind you about deadlines that were clearly established"** = "I shouldn't have to keep reminding you about deadlines that were already set"

Firm: "We have a fundamental issue with deadline management. This deadline was established [timeframe] ago, discussed repeatedly, and clearly documented. The fact that it surprised you indicates a serious gap in how you're managing your work. As a professional, you're expected to track your own commitments without requiring constant reminders. I need to see immediate improvement in deadline awareness. That means actively managing your calendar, setting your own alerts, and planning your work accordingly. If you can't reliably track when your work is due, we have a bigger problem than missed deadlines."

What you're communicating: "This is a major problem with how you handle deadlines. This deadline was set [timeframe] ago, talked about many times, and clearly written down. The fact that you were surprised by it shows a serious problem with how you manage your work. As a professional, you're supposed to track your own deadlines without needing constant reminders. You need to get immediately better at knowing when things are due. That means actively using your calendar, setting your own alerts, and planning your work. If you can't reliably remember when your work is due, we have a problem bigger than just missing deadlines."

Breaking it down:

- **"We have a fundamental issue with deadline management"** = "There's a basic problem with how you handle deadlines"

- **"This deadline was established [timeframe] ago, discussed repeatedly, and clearly documented"** = "This deadline was set long ago, talked about many times, and clearly written down"

- **"The fact that it surprised you indicates a serious gap in how you're managing your work"** = "You being surprised shows a serious problem with how you manage your work"

- **"As a professional, you're expected to track your own commitments without requiring constant reminders"** = "As a professional, you should remember your own deadlines without needing constant reminders"

- **"I need to see immediate improvement in deadline awareness"** = "You need to get better at knowing deadlines right away"

- **"That means actively managing your calendar, setting your own alerts, and planning your work accordingly"** = "That means using your calendar, setting alerts, and planning based on deadlines"

- **"If you can't reliably track when your work is due, we have a bigger problem than missed deadlines"** = "If you can't remember when things are due, we have a bigger problem than just being late"

Why This Works: You're identifying the root cause—they're not tracking their commitments—without saying they're incompetent. By emphasizing that the deadline was well-communicated, you're making it clear this is their responsibility, not yours. The firm version establishes that deadline awareness is a basic professional requirement, not an optional skill.

HR-APPROVED PHRASE COLLECTION

Instead of "You missed the deadline again"

A. "We have a pattern of missed deadlines we need to address." B. "Meeting deadlines needs to be a higher priority." C. "I need to see improvement in your ability to deliver on time." D. "Deadlines aren't suggestions—they're commitments." E. "Your track record with timelines has become a concern." F. "We need to discuss why deadlines have been challenging to meet." G. "I need advance notice if you can't meet a deadline, not day-of notifications."

Instead of "Why does this always happen to you?"

A. "Let's discuss how to prevent this pattern from continuing." B. "I'm seeing a recurring issue with timeline management." C. "This is becoming a consistent pattern we need to address." D. "We need to identify what's causing these repeated timeline issues." E. "I'm concerned about how frequently this is happening." F. "Let's figure out what's driving these consistent deadline challenges."

Instead of "You should have known better"

A. "This deadline was clearly communicated with [timeframe] notice." B. "We discussed this timeline multiple times." C. "The due date was established well in advance." D. "This was documented and confirmed in [meeting/email]." E. "You had [timeframe] to plan for this deadline." F. "This shouldn't have come as a surprise given our prior discussions."

Instead of "Stop making excuses"

A. "I need to see more focus on delivery and less on explanations after the fact." B. "Let's shift from discussing why things didn't happen to ensuring they do happen." C. "Other team members face similar obstacles and still meet deadlines." D. "I need proactive communication before deadlines, not reasons after." E. "The pattern of non-delivery is more concerning than individual circumstances." F. "I need to see accountability for managing around obstacles."

Instead of "You're terrible at planning"

A. "Let's work on building more accurate timeline estimates." B. "We need to improve how you're assessing task duration." C. "Your estimates consistently underestimate the actual time required." D. "Let's develop better systems for planning your work." E. "We need to find ways to make your timelines more realistic." F. "Time management and planning skills need development."

Instead of "You don't understand what urgent means"

A. "I need to see more responsiveness when deadlines are tight." B. "This needs to be treated as a priority." C. "The pace here needs to reflect the timeline we're working against." D. "When something is marked urgent, that needs to be reflected in your approach." E. "I'm not seeing appropriate urgency on time-sensitive work." F. "This deadline requires you to adjust your priorities accordingly."

Instead of "You're lying about your progress"

A. "There's a disconnect between your progress updates and the actual state of the work." B. "I need more accurate assessments of where things actually stand." C. "Let's ensure progress updates reflect reality, not optimism." D. "I need transparency about actual status, not what you hope it will be." E. "When you report progress, I need that to match what's actually complete." F. "We need honesty about timeline challenges before deadlines arrive."

Instead of "How can you be surprised by this deadline?"

A. "This deadline was clearly established and communicated." B. "I need you to take ownership of tracking your commitments." C. "Let's find a system to ensure deadlines aren't catching you off guard." D. "You're expected to manage your own deadline awareness." E. "This due date shouldn't have been a surprise." F. "I need you to proactively track when your work is due."

For setting expectations about advance notice

A. "If you can't meet a deadline, I need to know at least [X days] in advance." B. "Timeline concerns need to be flagged early, not at the last minute." C. "I expect early warning about potential deadline issues." D. "Last-minute notifications don't give us time to adjust plans." E. "Flag potential problems well before the deadline arrives." F. "I need advance notice, not day-of revelations about timeline issues."

For addressing chronic lateness

A. "This is now a pattern that's affecting team performance." B. "Continued deadline issues will impact your performance evaluation." C. "This has become a serious performance concern." D. "The frequency of missed deadlines is unacceptable." E. "This pattern of late delivery is affecting our ability to meet commitments." F. "We've reached the point where this is a critical performance issue."

When they need to improve estimation skills

A. "Let's work on making your timeline commitments more accurate." B. "You need to either improve your estimates or build in more buffer time." C. "Your projected timelines consistently don't match actual delivery." D. "We need to develop more realistic expectations about task duration." E. "Let's find ways to make your time estimates more reliable." F. "Going forward, all timeline commitments need to be more conservative."

For distinguishing between causes

A. "Help me understand if this is a planning issue, a capacity issue, or a prioritization issue." B. "Let's identify whether the problem is estimation, execution, or something else." C. "We need to figure out the root cause of these timeline challenges." D. "Is this about underestimating work, or about obstacles that arise?" E. "Let's determine what's driving these consistent deadline misses."

When vague updates aren't acceptable

A. "I need specific progress details, not general statements about working on it." B. "'Working on it' isn't helpful—I need to know what's complete and what's remaining." C. "Going forward, tell me specifically what you've finished, not just that you're making progress." D. "I need concrete status updates, not vague assurances." E. "Please provide specific milestones completed, not general progress statements."

To emphasize the downstream impact

A. "Your deadlines affect other people's work and project timelines." B. "When you miss deadlines, it creates a ripple effect on the team." C. "These commitments aren't just between us—they impact broader project coordination." D. "Your timeline affects my ability to deliver on commitments to others." E. "Deadline misses create problems for everyone depending on this work."

When they need better tracking systems

A. "You need to implement a system for tracking your commitments." B. "Find a method that works for you to stay on top of deadlines." C. "You're expected to maintain your own deadline awareness." D. "Set up reminders and tracking that ensure deadlines don't surprise you." E. "Take ownership of managing your calendar and work commitments."

Chapter 4 Quick Reference Box

Ten Essential Phrases for Missed Deadlines & Poor Time Management

1. "Deadlines aren't suggestions—they're commitments. I need advance notice if you can't meet one, not day-of notifications."

2. "There's a disconnect between your progress updates and actual status. I need transparency about where things really stand."

3. "This deadline was clearly established [timeframe] ago. Help me understand what prevented you from flagging concerns earlier."

4. "You consistently underestimate how long work takes. Going forward, either improve your estimates or build in significant buffer time."

5. "I'm seeing a pattern where obstacles prevent delivery. Other team members face similar challenges and still meet deadlines."

6. "When I check in, I need specific progress details—what's complete and what's remaining—not vague assurances about working on it."

7. "This has been on the calendar for [timeframe]. The fact that it surprised you indicates a gap in how you're tracking commitments."

8. "If something will prevent you from meeting a deadline, I need to know at least [X days] in advance so we can adjust plans."

9. "Your deadlines affect project timelines and other people's work. Meeting them is critical for team coordination."

10. "Continued deadline issues have become a serious performance concern that will affect your evaluation."

FIVE
LACK OF INITIATIVE & PASSIVE WORK STYLES

"I'd Like to See More Ownership" (Translation: Stop Waiting to Be Told What to Do)

Real Talk

Few things are more frustrating than managing someone who does exactly what you ask—and not one thing more. They wait for explicit instructions on the obvious next steps. They watch problems unfold without lifting a finger to address them. They complete Task A and then sit there, waiting for you to assign Task B, even when Task B is the logical next step that anyone with half a brain could figure out.

It's not that they're incompetent at executing specific instructions. Give them a clear task with defined parameters, and they'll do it. The problem is they have zero drive to think ahead, anticipate needs, or take action without being explicitly told. They're like highly trained robots who shut down the moment they complete their programmed task, incapable of looking around and thinking, "What should I do next?"

Maybe they're afraid of overstepping. Maybe they've learned that doing only what's asked protects them from criticism. Maybe they genuinely can't think proactively and need everything spelled out. Or maybe they just don't care enough to go beyond the bare minimum. Whatever the reason, the result is the same: you're spending mental energy directing someone who should be capable of directing themselves, and they're producing the absolute minimum required while technically fulfilling their job description.

You can't say "think for yourself," or "show some initiative," or "do I need to tell you to breathe too?" But you also can't keep micromanaging someone who should be operating with at least some degree of independence. This chapter gives you the language to address passivity and lack of ownership without being accused of having unreasonable expectations.

Five Principles for the Initiative Conversation

□ **Distinguish between lack of ability and lack of drive.** Can they not see what needs to be done, or do they see it and choose not to act? The conversation differs based on the answer.

□ **Set explicit expectations for proactive behavior.** Don't assume they know they should take initiative. Spell out what "ownership" and "proactive" mean in concrete terms.

□ **Connect initiative to impact.** Help them understand that waiting for direction doesn't just affect them—it slows down projects, burdens teammates, and limits their own growth.

□ **Give them permission to act.** Some people need explicit authorization to make decisions or take the next steps without checking first. Clarify where they have autonomy.

□ **Establish consequences for continued passivity.** Initiative is often viewed as optional. Make it clear that proactive work isn't a bonus—it's a requirement of the role.

Let's Get Real Scenarios

Scenario 1: They See the Problem, Do Nothing, Then Act Surprised When You're Upset

Situation: An obvious problem occurs—something goes wrong, a process breaks down, or an issue arises that clearly needs attention. The employee sees it happening, does nothing to address it, and later seems genuinely confused about why you're frustrated. They didn't think it was their responsibility, even though it obviously was within their scope.

What You're Thinking: "You literally watched this problem unfold and did nothing? You saw the issue, you knew it was a problem, and you just... waited for someone else to deal with it? How is that acceptable? At what point did you think, 'maybe I should do something about this'?"

What You Should Say:

Diplomatic: "I want to talk about what happened with [specific situation]. You were aware that [problem] was occurring, but I'm not seeing that you took any action to address it. Help me understand your thinking—did you not realize this needed attention, or was there a reason you didn't act on it? Going forward, I need you to take ownership when you see issues that fall within your scope, rather than waiting for someone to tell you to handle them."

What you're communicating: "We need to discuss what happened with [situation]. You knew [problem] was happening, but you didn't do anything about it. Help me understand why—did you not realize this needed to be fixed, or was there some reason you didn't do anything? From now on, when you see problems that are part of your job, you need to take care of them yourself instead of waiting for me to tell you."

Breaking it down:

- **"I want to talk about what happened with [specific situation]"** = "We need to discuss this specific problem"
- **"You were aware that [problem] was occurring"** = "You knew this problem was happening"
- **"But I'm not seeing that you took any action to address it"** = "But you didn't do anything about it"
- **"Help me understand your thinking—did you not realize this needed attention, or was there a reason you didn't act on it?"** = "Explain why—did you not know it needed to be fixed, or did you choose not to act?"
- **"Going forward, I need you to take ownership when you see issues that fall within your scope"** = "From now on, handle problems that are part of your job"
- **"Rather than waiting for someone to tell you to handle them"** = "Instead of waiting for instructions"

More Direct: "We have a problem with how you responded to [situation]. You saw [issue] happening and didn't take action. That's not acceptable. When problems arise within your area of responsibility, I expect you to address them proactively, not wait for someone to notice and assign you the task. This isn't about overstepping—this is basic ownership of your work. You need to see problems as your responsibility to solve, not opportunities to wait for direction."

What you're communicating: "There's a problem with how you handled [situation]. You saw [issue] and did nothing. That's not okay. When problems happen in your area, you need to fix them without waiting for someone to tell you. This isn't about doing things you shouldn't—this is basic responsibility for your own work. You need to see problems as your job to fix, not things to ignore until someone tells you what to do."

Breaking it down:

- **"We have a problem with how you responded to [situation]"** = "How you handled this situation is a problem"

- **"You saw [issue] happening and didn't take action"** = "You saw the problem and did nothing"
- **"That's not acceptable"** = "That's not okay"
- **"When problems arise within your area of responsibility, I expect you to address them proactively"** = "When problems happen in your area, fix them without waiting"
- **"Not wait for someone to notice and assign you the task"** = "Don't wait for someone to tell you to do it"
- **"This isn't about overstepping—this is basic ownership of your work"** = "This isn't doing too much—this is basic responsibility"
- **"You need to see problems as your responsibility to solve, not opportunities to wait for direction"** = "You need to see problems as your job to fix, not things to ignore until told"

Firm: "I need to be direct about a serious issue. When [problem] occurred, you saw it happening and chose not to act. That represents a fundamental failure of ownership and professional judgment. Part of your role is recognizing when issues need attention and addressing them—not waiting for explicit instructions on every problem that arises. This passive approach is unacceptable. Going forward, when you see problems within your scope, you're expected to take initiative to resolve them. If you're unclear about your scope of authority, we need to discuss that now, because inaction when action is clearly needed is a performance issue."

What you're communicating: "Let me be blunt about a serious problem. When [problem] happened, you saw it and chose to do nothing. That shows a major failure to take responsibility and use good judgment. Part of your job is noticing when things need attention and fixing them—not waiting for me to tell you to handle every single problem. This passive behavior is unacceptable. From now on, when you see problems in your area, you're expected to take action to fix them. If you're not clear about what you're allowed to do, we need to talk about that right now, because doing nothing when action is obviously needed is a performance problem."

Breaking it down:

- **"I need to be direct about a serious issue"** = "Let me be blunt about a major problem"
- **"You saw it happening and chose not to act"** = "You saw it and chose to do nothing"
- **"That represents a fundamental failure of ownership and professional judgment"** = "That shows a basic failure to take responsibility and use good judgment"
- **"Part of your role is recognizing when issues need attention and addressing them"** = "Part of your job is noticing problems and fixing them"
- **"Not waiting for explicit instructions on every problem that arises"** = "Not waiting to be told about every single problem"
- **"This passive approach is unacceptable"** = "This inactive behavior is not okay"
- **"When you see problems within your scope, you're expected to take initiative to resolve them"** = "When you see problems in your area, you should act to fix them"
- **"If you're unclear about your scope of authority, we need to discuss that now"** = "If you don't know what you're allowed to do, we need to talk about it now"
- **"Because inaction when action is clearly needed is a performance issue"** = "Because doing nothing when something obviously needs to be done is a job performance problem"

Why This Works: You're making it explicit that seeing a problem and doing nothing is not acceptable. By asking if they understood it was their responsibility, you're raising the issue of whether this is a scope issue or an initiative issue. The firm version establishes that proactive problem-solving is a job requirement, and not optional.

Scenario 2: Waiting for Explicit Instructions on Common-Sense Tasks

Situation: The employee completes an assigned task and then stops, waiting for you to tell them the obvious next step. Or they encounter a routine situation and come to you for instructions on something that clearly follows standard procedure or basic logic. They need their hand held through things that should be automatic.

What You're Thinking: "Are you kidding me right now? You just finished Task A. Task B is the logical next step. Everyone knows that. Why are you standing here waiting for me to tell you to do the thing that obviously comes next? Can you really not figure out what to do without me spelling out every single step?"

What You Should Say:

Diplomatic: "I want to help you develop more independence in your work. When you completed [Task A], the natural next step would be [Task B]. In the future, when you finish a task, take a moment to think about what logically comes next before checking with me. If you're genuinely unsure, that's fine—but if there's an obvious next step, you should feel empowered to move forward with it."

What you're communicating: "I want to help you work more independently. After you finished [Task A], the obvious next step was [Task B]. From now on, when you finish something, think about what comes next before asking me. If you really don't know, that's okay—but if the next step is obvious, you should just go ahead and do it without checking with me."

Breaking it down:

- **"I want to help you develop more independence in your work"** = "I want you to work more on your own"
- **"When you completed [Task A], the natural next step would be [Task B]"** = "After finishing [Task A], the obvious next thing is [Task B]"

- **"In the future, when you finish a task, take a moment to think about what logically comes next"** = "From now on, after finishing something, think about what should happen next"
- **"Before checking with me"** = "Before asking me"
- **"If you're genuinely unsure, that's fine"** = "If you really don't know, that's okay"
- **"But if there's an obvious next step, you should feel empowered to move forward with it"** = "But if it's obvious what's next, just do it without asking"

More Direct: "I need to address something: you're asking for direction on tasks that should be straightforward. When you finish [X], [Y] is the logical next step—you shouldn't need me to tell you that. Part of operating in this role is being able to identify obvious next steps and take them without waiting for explicit instruction. I need you to develop that judgment and act on it. If something is truly ambiguous or outside normal procedure, ask. But routine next steps should be handled independently."

What you're communicating: "We need to talk about something: you're asking me for instructions on things that should be obvious. After you finish [X], [Y] is the clear next step—you shouldn't need me to tell you. Part of doing this job is being able to figure out obvious next steps and do them without waiting to be told. You need to develop that ability and use it. If something is really unclear or unusual, then ask. But normal next steps you should handle on your own."

Breaking it down:

- **"I need to address something: you're asking for direction on tasks that should be straightforward"** = "We need to discuss: you're asking me about things that should be obvious"
- **"When you finish [X], [Y] is the logical next step—you shouldn't need me to tell you that"** = "After doing [X], [Y] is clearly next—I shouldn't have to tell you"

- **"Part of operating in this role is being able to identify obvious next steps and take them"** = "Part of this job is figuring out clear next steps and doing them"
- **"Without waiting for explicit instruction"** = "Without waiting to be told"
- **"I need you to develop that judgment and act on it"** = "You need to develop that ability and use it"
- **"If something is truly ambiguous or outside normal procedure, ask"** = "If something is really unclear or unusual, then ask"
- **"But routine next steps should be handled independently"** = "But normal next steps you should do yourself"

Firm: "We need to talk about your need for constant direction. You're regularly coming to me for instructions on tasks and next steps that should be self-evident. When you complete [routine task], the next action is obvious—it's part of the standard workflow. Your role requires the ability to think ahead, identify logical next steps, and execute them without needing to be walked through every phase. I expect you to take initiative on routine work going forward. If you're unable to identify obvious next steps independently, that's a capability concern we need to address."

What you're communicating: "We have to discuss how much you need me to tell you what to do. You keep asking me for instructions on things that should be obvious. When you finish [routine task], what comes next is clear—it's part of the normal process. Your job requires you to think ahead, figure out obvious next steps, and do them without being guided through everything. I expect you to take action on routine work from now on. If you can't figure out obvious next steps on your own, that's a serious problem with your ability to do this job."

Breaking it down:

- **"We need to talk about your need for constant direction"** = "We have to discuss how much you need me to tell you what to do"

- **"You're regularly coming to me for instructions on tasks and next steps that should be self-evident"** = "You keep asking me about things that should be obvious"
- **"When you complete [routine task], the next action is obvious—it's part of the standard workflow"** = "After finishing [routine task], what's next is clear—it's part of the normal process"
- **"Your role requires the ability to think ahead, identify logical next steps, and execute them"** = "Your job needs you to think ahead, figure out obvious next steps, and do them"
- **"Without needing to be walked through every phase"** = "Without being guided through everything"
- **"I expect you to take initiative on routine work going forward"** = "You need to take action on normal work from now on"
- **"If you're unable to identify obvious next steps independently, that's a capability concern"** = "If you can't figure out clear next steps yourself, that's a serious problem"

Why This Works: You're drawing the distinction between genuine uncertainty and needing hand-holding on obvious tasks. By calling out specific examples where the next step should have been clear, you're demonstrating that this is about initiative, not ambiguous situations. The firm version establishes that this level of dependence is below what the role requires.

Scenario 3: "I Didn't Think That Was My Job" (It Obviously Was)

Situation: Something clearly within the employee's scope of responsibility doesn't get done. When you ask about it, they say they didn't think it was their job—despite the fact that it's obviously related to their core responsibilities or is a natural extension of their role.

What You're Thinking: "You didn't think it was your job? How could it possibly be anyone else's job? This is literally what you were hired to do. Did you think someone else would magically handle the thing that is explicitly your responsibility? What did you think your job was?"

What You Should Say:

Diplomatic: "I want to make sure we're aligned on your scope of responsibility. When [task/issue] came up, I expected that it would fall within your area, but you indicated you didn't see it as your responsibility. Help me understand where the confusion is—what's your understanding of what falls within your role? Let's clarify the boundaries so you know when to take ownership versus when to escalate."

What you're communicating: "I need to make sure we both understand what you're responsible for. When [task/issue] happened, I thought that was part of your job, but you said you didn't think it was. Help me understand the confusion—what do you think is part of your job? Let's make clear what you should handle yourself versus when to ask someone else."

Breaking it down:

- **"I want to make sure we're aligned on your scope of responsibility"** = "I need to know we agree on what you're responsible for"
- **"When [task/issue] came up, I expected that it would fall within your area"** = "When [task/issue] happened, I thought that was your job"
- **"But you indicated you didn't see it as your responsibility"** = "But you said it wasn't your job"
- **"Help me understand where the confusion is"** = "Help me understand the misunderstanding"
- **"What's your understanding of what falls within your role?"** = "What do you think is part of your job?"
- **"Let's clarify the boundaries so you know when to take ownership versus when to escalate"** = "Let's make clear what you should handle versus when to involve others"

More Direct: "We need to clarify job responsibilities. [Task/issue] is clearly within your scope—it's a core part of your role. The fact that you didn't think it was your job concerns me. This isn't a gray area or an edge case. When you see something that's directly related to your primary responsibilities, you need to take ownership of it. I shouldn't have to explicitly assign you every task that falls within your job description. Part of professional responsibility is recognizing what needs to be done within your area and doing it."

What you're communicating: "We need to be clear about what your job is. [Task/issue] is definitely your job—it's a main part of your role. The fact that you didn't think so worries me. This isn't unclear or questionable. When you see something that's directly related to your main responsibilities, you need to handle it. I shouldn't have to specifically assign you every task that's part of your job description. Part of being professional is recognizing what needs to be done in your area and doing it."

Breaking it down:

- **"We need to clarify job responsibilities"** = "We need to be clear about what your job is"
- **"[Task/issue] is clearly within your scope—it's a core part of your role"** = "[Task/issue] is definitely your job—it's a main part of your role"
- **"The fact that you didn't think it was your job concerns me"** = "You not thinking it was your job worries me"
- **"This isn't a gray area or an edge case"** = "This isn't unclear or questionable"
- **"When you see something that's directly related to your primary responsibilities, you need to take ownership of it"** = "When something is clearly related to your main job, you need to handle it"
- **"I shouldn't have to explicitly assign you every task that falls within your job description"** = "I shouldn't have to tell you to do every single thing that's part of your job"

- **"Part of professional responsibility is recognizing what needs to be done within your area and doing it"** = "Part of being professional is seeing what needs to be done in your area and doing it"

Firm: "I need to be very direct: [task/issue] is absolutely within your job responsibilities. There's no ambiguity here—this is core to your role. The fact that you didn't recognize this as yours to handle indicates either a misunderstanding of your job scope or a reluctance to take ownership. Either way, we need to correct this immediately. You're expected to proactively handle anything that falls within your area of responsibility, not wait to be assigned specific tasks. If you're unclear about what your role encompasses, tell me now, because 'I didn't think that was my job' isn't acceptable when it clearly is."

What you're communicating: "Let me be very clear: [task/issue] is definitely your job. There's no confusion here—this is a main part of your role. You not recognizing this as your responsibility shows either that you don't understand your job or that you don't want to take ownership. Either way, we need to fix this now. You're supposed to handle anything in your area without being assigned specific tasks. If you don't understand what your role includes, tell me now, because 'I didn't think that was my job' doesn't work when it clearly is."

Breaking it down:

- **"I need to be very direct: [task/issue] is absolutely within your job responsibilities"** = "Let me be clear: [task/issue] is definitely your job"
- **"There's no ambiguity here—this is core to your role"** = "There's no confusion—this is a main part of your job"
- **"The fact that you didn't recognize this as yours to handle"** = "You not recognizing this as your responsibility"
- **"Indicates either a misunderstanding of your job scope or a reluctance to take ownership"** = "Shows either you don't understand your job or you don't want to take responsibility"

- **"Either way, we need to correct this immediately"** = "Either way, we need to fix this now"
- **"You're expected to proactively handle anything that falls within your area of responsibility"** = "You should handle anything in your area without waiting"
- **"Not wait to be assigned specific tasks"** = "Not wait to be given specific tasks"
- **"If you're unclear about what your role encompasses, tell me now"** = "If you don't understand what your job includes, tell me now"
- **"Because 'I didn't think that was my job' isn't acceptable when it clearly is"** = "Because 'I didn't think that was my job' doesn't work when it obviously is"

Why This Works: You're establishing that this falls clearly within their scope, not in some ambiguous zone. By offering to clarify boundaries, you're giving them a chance to surface genuine confusion while making it clear this particular task isn't debatable. The firm version makes explicit that claiming ignorance of core responsibilities is unacceptable.

Scenario 4: Zero Proactive Problem-Solving

Situation: The employee encounters obstacles, challenges, or questions and immediately comes to you rather than attempting to solve anything themselves. They don't try to figure it out, research options, or think through solutions. Every bump in the road becomes your problem to solve.

What You're Thinking: "Did you try literally anything before coming to me? Did you Google it? Did you check the documentation? Did you think about it for even five seconds? Why am I solving problems that you should be able to handle? Am I your boss or your personal problem-solver?"

What You Should Say:

Diplomatic: "I want to help you build stronger problem-solving skills. When you encounter an obstacle, I'd like you to take some time to explore potential solutions before bringing it to me. That might mean checking documentation, researching similar situations, or thinking through a few options. When you do come to me, let me know what you've already tried or considered—that helps me understand the issue better and makes our conversations more productive."

What you're communicating: "I want to help you get better at solving problems yourself. When you hit a roadblock, I want you to try to figure out solutions before asking me. That could mean looking at our guides, finding similar examples, or thinking about a few possible answers. When you do ask me, tell me what you've already tried—that helps me understand better and makes our discussions more useful."

Breaking it down:

- **"I want to help you build stronger problem-solving skills"** = "I want to help you get better at solving problems"
- **"When you encounter an obstacle, I'd like you to take some time to explore potential solutions before bringing it to me"** = "When you hit a problem, try to figure out solutions before asking me"
- **"That might mean checking documentation, researching similar situations, or thinking through a few options"** = "That could mean reading guides, looking at examples, or considering possible answers"
- **"When you do come to me, let me know what you've already tried or considered"** = "When you do ask me, tell me what you've tried"
- **"That helps me understand the issue better and makes our conversations more productive"** = "That helps me understand better and makes our discussions more useful"

More Direct: "We need to change how you approach problem-solving. You're coming to me with every obstacle rather than attempting to work through things yourself first. I need you to invest effort in solving problems independently before escalating. That means trying to find answers, thinking through options, and making reasonable attempts at resolution. My role is to help when you're truly stuck—not to be your first resource for every challenge you encounter. You need to develop more self-sufficiency."

What you're communicating: "We need to change how you handle problems. You're asking me about every obstacle instead of trying to figure things out first. You need to try to solve problems yourself before asking me. That means looking for answers, thinking about options, and trying reasonable solutions. I'm here to help when you're really stuck—not to be the first person you ask for every challenge. You need to be more independent."

Breaking it down:

- **"We need to change how you approach problem-solving"** = "We need to change how you handle problems"
- **"You're coming to me with every obstacle rather than attempting to work through things yourself first"** = "You're asking me about every problem instead of trying to figure it out first"
- **"I need you to invest effort in solving problems independently before escalating"** = "You need to try solving problems yourself before asking me"
- **"That means trying to find answers, thinking through options, and making reasonable attempts at resolution"** = "That means looking for solutions, considering choices, and trying to fix things"
- **"My role is to help when you're truly stuck—not to be your first resource for every challenge you encounter"** = "I'm here for when you're really stuck—not as the first person you ask every time"
- **"You need to develop more self-sufficiency"** = "You need to be more independent"

Firm: "I need to address your reliance on me for problem-solving. Every time you hit an obstacle, you're immediately coming to me rather than making any attempt to resolve it yourself. That's not sustainable, and it's not appropriate for your level. I expect you to apply critical thinking, research solutions, and make attempts at resolution before escalating issues. Part of your job is figuring things out, not outsourcing every challenge to me. Going forward, unless there's a genuine emergency or you've exhausted reasonable options, I expect you to spend time working on solutions independently. This learned helplessness needs to stop."

What you're communicating: "We need to discuss how much you depend on me to solve problems. Every time you face a challenge, you immediately ask me instead of trying to fix it yourself. That's not workable, and it's not right for your position. I expect you to think critically, look for solutions, and try to fix things before asking me. Part of your job is solving problems, not giving every challenge to me to solve. From now on, unless it's a real emergency or you've tried everything reasonable, you need to spend time working on solutions yourself. This pattern of helplessness has to stop."

Breaking it down:

- **"I need to address your reliance on me for problem-solving"** = "We need to discuss how much you depend on me"
- **"Every time you hit an obstacle, you're immediately coming to me"** = "Every time you face a challenge, you ask me right away"
- **"Rather than making any attempt to resolve it yourself"** = "Instead of trying to fix it yourself"
- **"That's not sustainable and it's not appropriate for your level"** = "That can't continue and it's not right for your position"
- **"I expect you to apply critical thinking, research solutions, and make attempts at resolution before escalating issues"** = "You should think critically, look for solutions, and try to fix things before asking me"

- **"Part of your job is figuring things out, not outsourcing every challenge to me"** = "Part of your job is solving problems, not giving every challenge to me"
- **"Going forward, unless there's a genuine emergency or you've exhausted reasonable options"** = "From now on, unless it's a real emergency or you've tried everything"
- **"I expect you to spend time working on solutions independently"** = "You need to work on solutions yourself"
- **"This learned helplessness needs to stop"** = "This pattern of helplessness has to stop"

Why This Works: You're establishing that coming to you should be the last step, not the first. By asking them to share what they've tried when they do escalate, you're creating accountability for attempting solutions first. The firm version calls out learned helplessness directly and makes clear that self-sufficiency is a job requirement.

Scenario 5: They Complete Only What's Explicitly Asked

Situation: You assign a project or task, and the employee does exactly that—nothing more, nothing less. They don't consider related tasks, they don't think about what might be needed next, and they don't go one millimeter beyond the explicit scope. Technically, they've done what you asked, but anyone with initiative would have done more.

What You're Thinking: "Really? You completed this one narrow task and called it done? Did you not think about the five related things that obviously need to happen? Did you not consider what the next step would be? Does 'doing your job' mean doing only the absolute bare minimum you're explicitly told to do?"

What You Should Say:

Diplomatic: "I want to talk about how we approach projects. When you completed [specific task], which met the explicit ask, and I appreciate that. However, there were related elements—[examples]—that would have been natural extensions of that work. Going forward, I'd like you to think more broadly about projects: what else might be needed, what the next logical steps are, and what would make the work more complete. Look for opportunities to add value beyond just the literal ask."

What you're communicating: "Let's discuss how we handle projects. When you finished [specific task], you did what I asked, and that's good. But there were related things—[examples]—that naturally go with that work. From now on, I want you to think bigger about projects: what else might be needed, what should happen next, and what would make the work better. Look for chances to contribute more than just exactly what I asked for."

Breaking it down:

- **"I want to talk about how we approach projects"** = "Let's discuss how we handle projects"
- **"When you completed [specific task], that met the explicit ask, and I appreciate that"** = "When you finished [task], you did what I asked, which is good"
- **"However, there were related elements—[examples]—that would have been natural extensions of that work"** = "But there were related things—[examples]—that naturally go with that work"
- **"Going forward, I'd like you to think more broadly about projects"** = "From now on, I want you to think bigger about projects"
- **"What else might be needed, what the next logical steps are, and what would make the work more complete"** = "What else is needed, what comes next, and what would make it better"
- **"Look for opportunities to add value beyond just the literal ask"** = "Find chances to contribute more than just what I specifically asked"

More Direct: "We need to discuss your approach to assignments. You're fulfilling the letter of what's asked, but not thinking beyond it. When you completed [task], there were obvious related needs—[examples]—that you could have addressed. I need to see you taking a more holistic view: when you get an assignment, think about the broader goal, anticipate what else might be needed, and take initiative on related work. Meeting the minimum requirement isn't the goal—delivering comprehensive, thoughtful work is."

What you're communicating: "We need to talk about how you do assignments. You're doing exactly what's asked but not thinking past that. When you finished [task], there were obvious related things—[examples]—that you could have done. You need to think more broadly: when you get an assignment, think about the bigger goal, predict what else is needed, and take action on related work. Just meeting the basic requirement isn't enough—delivering complete, thoughtful work is what matters."

Breaking it down:

- **"We need to discuss your approach to assignments"** = "We need to talk about how you do assignments"
- **"You're fulfilling the letter of what's asked but not thinking beyond it"** = "You're doing exactly what's asked but not thinking past it"
- **"When you completed [task], there were obvious related needs—[examples]"** = "When you finished [task], there were clear related things"
- **"That you could have addressed"** = "That you could have done"
- **"I need to see you taking a more holistic view"** = "You need to think more broadly"
- **"When you get an assignment, think about the broader goal, anticipate what else might be needed"** = "When you get work, think about the bigger goal and predict what else is needed"
- **"And take initiative on related work"** = "And take action on related tasks"
- **"Meeting the minimum requirement isn't the goal—delivering comprehensive, thoughtful work is"** = "Just meeting the basic requirement isn't enough—complete, thoughtful work is what matters"

Firm: "I need to be frank about your work approach. You're consistently doing exactly what's asked and nothing more. When you completed [task], you stopped without addressing [related elements] that any reasonable person would see as connected. This bare-minimum approach isn't what this role requires. I need proactive, thoughtful work—not someone who needs every single element spelled out explicitly. Going forward, when you receive an assignment, you're expected to think critically about what else is needed, what the end goal requires, and what would make the deliverable complete. If you're only capable of executing narrow, explicit instructions, we need to discuss whether this role is the right fit."

What you're communicating: "Let me be direct about how you work. You keep doing exactly what's asked and nothing more. When you finished [task], you stopped without doing [related things] that anyone would see as connected. This minimal approach isn't what this job needs. I need proactive, thoughtful work—not someone who needs every detail spelled out. From now on, when you get an assignment, you should think about what else is needed, what the goal requires, and what would make it complete. If you can only follow narrow, specific instructions, we need to discuss if this is the right job for you."

Breaking it down:

- **"I need to be frank about your work approach"** = "Let me be direct about how you work"
- **"You're consistently doing exactly what's asked and nothing more"** = "You keep doing exactly what's asked and nothing else"
- **"When you completed [task], you stopped without addressing [related elements]"** = "When you finished [task], you stopped without doing [related things]"
- **"That any reasonable person would see as connected"** = "That anyone would see as related"
- **"This bare-minimum approach isn't what this role requires"** = "This minimal approach isn't what this job needs"

- **"I need proactive, thoughtful work—not someone who needs every single element spelled out explicitly"** = "I need proactive, thoughtful work—not someone who needs every detail explained"
- **"Going forward, when you receive an assignment, you're expected to think critically"** = "From now on, when you get work, you should think carefully"
- **"About what else is needed, what the end goal requires, and what would make the deliverable complete"** = "About what else is needed, what the goal requires, and what makes it complete"
- **"If you're only capable of executing narrow, explicit instructions"** = "If you can only follow specific, narrow instructions"
- **"We need to discuss whether this role is the right fit"** = "We need to talk about if this is the right job for you"

Why This Works: You're acknowledging they did what was asked while making it clear that's insufficient. By providing specific examples of what they missed, you're showing them what initiative looks like. The firm version establishes that thinking beyond explicit instructions is a fundamental job requirement, not a bonus skill.

Scenario 6: They Don't Anticipate or Plan Ahead

Situation: The employee operates in a perpetual state of the present moment. They don't think about what's coming, don't prepare for predictable next steps, and don't anticipate needs. Everything is reactive because they never look beyond the immediate task in front of them.

What You're Thinking: "Do you not have the ability to think even one step ahead? We've done this process ten times. You know what happens next. Why are you waiting until it arrives to start thinking about it? Can you not see around corners even slightly? What happens in your brain between tasks?"

What You Should Say:

Diplomatic: "I'd like to work with you on developing forward-thinking skills. I'm noticing that when we move through [process/project], each phase seems to be addressed only when we arrive at it rather than being anticipated. For example, [specific instance]. Thinking ahead about what's coming allows you to prepare, gather what you need, and work more efficiently. Let's talk about how you can build that into your workflow—maybe setting aside time to plan ahead or creating checklists of upcoming needs."

What you're communicating: "I want to help you develop the ability to think ahead. I see that as we go through [process/project], you only deal with each phase when you get to it instead of preparing ahead. For example, [specific instance]. Thinking about what's coming lets you get ready, collect what you need, and work better. Let's discuss how you can do this—maybe planning time to think ahead or making lists of what's coming up."

Breaking it down:

- **"I'd like to work with you on developing forward-thinking skills"** = "I want to help you learn to think ahead"
- **"I'm noticing that when we move through [process/project], each phase seems to be addressed only when we arrive at it"** = "I see that during [process/project], you only handle each step when you reach it"
- **"Rather than being anticipated"** = "Instead of preparing for it ahead of time"
- **"For example, [specific instance]"** = "Like [specific example]"
- **"Thinking ahead about what's coming allows you to prepare, gather what you need, and work more efficiently"** = "Planning for what's next lets you get ready, collect what you need, and work better"
- **"Let's talk about how you can build that into your workflow"** = "Let's discuss how to make this part of how you work"
- **"Maybe setting aside time to plan ahead or creating**

checklists of upcoming needs" = "Perhaps scheduling planning time or making lists of what's coming"

More Direct: "We need to address your lack of forward planning. You're consistently reacting to things as they happen rather than anticipating and preparing. When we work through [process], the steps are predictable—you should be thinking about what's coming and preparing for it, not waiting until you're there. This reactive approach creates inefficiency and missed opportunities to work smarter. I need you to start looking ahead: when you complete one phase, think about what's next and what you'll need for it."

What you're communicating: "We need to fix your lack of planning ahead. You keep reacting to things as they happen instead of preparing. When we go through [process], the steps are known—you should think about what's coming and get ready for it, not wait until you're there. This reactive way of working is inefficient and means you miss chances to work smarter. You need to start looking forward: when you finish one step, think about what's next and what you'll need."

Breaking it down:

- **"We need to address your lack of forward planning"** = "We need to fix your lack of planning ahead"
- **"You're consistently reacting to things as they happen rather than anticipating and preparing"** = "You keep responding to things as they happen instead of predicting and preparing"
- **"When we work through [process], the steps are predictable"** = "When we do [process], the steps are known"
- **"You should be thinking about what's coming and preparing for it"** = "You should think about what's next and get ready"
- **"Not waiting until you're there"** = "Not waiting until you reach that point"
- **"This reactive approach creates inefficiency and missed opportunities to work smarter"** = "This reactive way causes inefficiency and missed chances to work better"

- **"I need you to start looking ahead: when you complete one phase, think about what's next and what you'll need for it"** = "You need to look forward: after finishing one step, think about what comes next and what you'll need"

Firm: "I need to be direct about a critical gap: you're not demonstrating the ability to think ahead and plan proactively. You work exclusively in the present moment, addressing each task only when it's immediately in front of you. That approach doesn't work for this role. I need someone who can anticipate needs, prepare for upcoming phases, and work strategically. When you're in [situation], you should already be thinking about what's ahead, like [next phase]. If you can't start thinking ahead, you'll miss important steps that are essential to help you be prepared. This isn't optional—anticipating and planning ahead is a core requirement of this position."

What you're communicating: "Let me be clear about a major problem: you're not showing the ability to think ahead and plan. You only work on what's right in front of you, dealing with each task only when it's immediate. That doesn't work for this job. I need someone who can predict needs, prepare for what's coming, and work strategically. When you're in [situation], you should already be thinking about [next phase], so you're on top of your preparation. This isn't an optional process—anticipating and planning ahead is essential for this job."

Breaking it down:

- **"I need to be direct about a critical gap"** = "Let me be clear about a major problem"
- **"You're not demonstrating the ability to think ahead and plan proactively"** = "You're not showing you can think ahead and plan"
- **"You work exclusively in the present moment"** = "You only work on what's right now"
- **"Addressing each task only when it's immediately in front of you"** = "Dealing with each task only when it's immediate"

- **"That approach doesn't work for this role"** = "That method doesn't work for this job"
- **"I need someone who can anticipate needs, prepare for upcoming phases, and work strategically"** = "I need someone who can predict needs, prepare for what's coming, and work strategically"
- **"When you're in [situation], you should already be thinking about [next phase]"** = "During [situation], you should already be considering [next phase]"
- **"If you can't develop that forward-thinking capability"** = "If you can't develop that ability to think ahead"
- **"You'll continue to operate inefficiently and miss important preparation"** = "You'll keep working inefficiently and missing important preparation"
- **"This isn't optional—anticipating and planning ahead is a core requirement of this position"** = "This isn't optional—thinking ahead and planning is essential for this job"

Why This Works: You're identifying the specific problem—lack of anticipation—and providing concrete examples of what that looks like. By explaining the benefits of forward thinking, you're showing them why this matters beyond just "I said so." The firm version makes explicit that this is a capability issue that affects their effectiveness in the role.

HR-APPROVED PHRASE COLLECTION

Instead of "Think for yourself"

1. "I'd like to see you take more ownership of identifying solutions."
2. "Part of your role is determining appropriate next steps independently."
3. "I need you to develop stronger independent judgment."
4. "You should feel empowered to make decisions within your scope."

5. "I expect you to take initiative on routine matters."
6. "Work through potential solutions before escalating issues."
7. "Your role requires proactive problem-solving skills."
8. "I need to see more self-directed decision-making."

Instead of "Show some initiative"

1. "I'd like to see more proactive behavior in your work."
2. "Look for opportunities to add value beyond the explicit ask."
3. "Take ownership of identifying what needs to be done."
4. "I need you to be more forward-thinking in your approach."
5. "Anticipate needs rather than waiting to be told."
6. "I expect you to identify and address issues without prompting."
7. "Your role requires a more proactive mindset."
8. "Take initiative on tasks that fall within your responsibility."

Instead of "Stop waiting to be told what to do"

1. "I need you to work more independently without constant direction."
2. "You should be able to identify obvious next steps without checking with me."
3. "I expect you to move forward on clear tasks without requiring explicit instruction."
4. "Develop the ability to determine appropriate actions without guidance."
5. "You're expected to operate with greater independence."
6. "I shouldn't need to walk you through every phase of routine work."
7. "Take action on straightforward next steps without waiting for direction."

Instead of "Why didn't you do anything about this?"

1. "When you see issues within your scope, I expect you to address them."
2. "Help me understand why you didn't take action on this."
3. "This fell within your area of responsibility—what prevented you from handling it?"
4. "I'm concerned that you saw this problem and didn't act on it."
5. "When issues arise in your area, you should take ownership of resolving them."
6. "Walking past problems without addressing them isn't acceptable."

Instead of "This is obviously your job"

1. "This falls clearly within your core responsibilities."
2. "This is a fundamental part of your role."
3. "This is exactly the type of work your position encompasses."
4. "This is central to your job description."
5. "This sits squarely within your scope of responsibility."
6. "There shouldn't be ambiguity about whether this is your responsibility."

Instead of "Figure it out yourself"

1. "I need you to invest effort in solving this independently first."
2. "Try to work through potential solutions before bringing this to me."
3. "Apply critical thinking and research to find solutions."
4. "Make reasonable attempts at resolution before escalating."
5. "You should exhaust your own problem-solving resources first."
6. "Demonstrate what you've tried before seeking my input."

Instead of "Do more than the bare minimum"

1. "I need you to think beyond just the literal ask."
2. "Consider what else might be needed to fully address this."
3. "Look at the broader context, not just the narrow task."
4. "Think about what would make this work truly complete."
5. "Meeting minimum requirements isn't the goal—delivering comprehensive work is."
6. "Consider related elements that naturally extend from this work."

Instead of "Why do I have to spell everything out?"

1. "I need you to connect the dots without explicit instruction on every step."
2. "You should be able to identify logical next steps independently."
3. "I expect you to fill in obvious gaps without needing direction."
4. "Routine workflow shouldn't require detailed guidance at every phase."
5. "Part of your role is determining what needs to happen without being told."

Instead of "You're completely passive"

1. "I need to see more active engagement with your work."
2. "Your approach is too reactive—I need you to be more proactive."
3. "You're waiting for things to happen rather than making them happen."
4. "I need you to take a more active role in driving your work forward."
5. "Move from responding to situations to anticipating and addressing them."
6. "Your work style needs to shift from passive to proactive."

Instead of "You lack drive"

1. "I need to see more self-motivation in your work."
2. "Take more initiative in advancing your projects."
3. "I'm looking for greater ownership and drive."
4. "Your work would benefit from more internal motivation."
5. "I need you to be more self-directed and engaged."
6. "Show more enthusiasm for taking on challenges and responsibilities."

When they need permission to act

1. "You're authorized to make decisions on [specific scope]."
2. "You don't need to check with me on routine matters—you have the authority to proceed."
3. "I'm giving you the autonomy to handle [types of situations] independently."
4. "Within [boundaries], you should feel empowered to act without approval."
5. "You have my trust to make calls on [scope] without checking in first."

For anticipating needs

1. "Think ahead about what's coming and prepare accordingly."
2. "Anticipate what will be needed in the next phase."
3. "Look forward to what's required rather than only addressing what's immediate."
4. "Build forward-thinking into your workflow."
5. "Prepare for predictable next steps before they arrive."
6. "Consider what you'll need before you need it."

When they need to recognize patterns

1. "Notice the patterns in our workflow and anticipate accordingly."
2. "After doing this [X times], you should recognize the standard progression."
3. "This follows a predictable pattern—use that to guide your actions."
4. "The sequence here is consistent—internalize it so you can work more independently."

For taking ownership

1. "Take ownership of outcomes, not just tasks."
2. "Own the entire scope of your responsibility, not just individual assignments."
3. "Treat this work as yours to drive, not mine to direct."
4. "Take responsibility for ensuring this succeeds."
5. "Own the problem and the solution."

When learned helplessness is the issue

1. "You're more capable than you're demonstrating—I need to see that capability in action."
2. "Stop defaulting to seeking help and start applying your own judgment."
3. "You have the skills to solve these problems—use them."
4. "This pattern of immediate escalation needs to stop."
5. "Build confidence by working through challenges independently."

Chapter 5 Quick Reference Box

Ten Essential Phrases for Lack of Initiative & Passive Work Styles

1. "When you see issues within your scope, I expect you to address them proactively—not wait for explicit direction."

2. "Part of your role is identifying obvious next steps and executing them independently, without checking in on routine matters."

3. "I need you to invest effort in solving problems yourself first—research options, think through solutions—before escalating to me."

4. "Think beyond the literal ask: consider related needs, anticipate what's next, and deliver comprehensive work, not bare minimum."

5. "When you encounter obstacles, make reasonable attempts at resolution before bringing them to me. Show me what you've tried when you do escalate."

6. "This task is clearly within your core responsibilities. 'I didn't think that was my job' isn't acceptable when it obviously is."

7. "I need you to take ownership of outcomes, not just complete assigned tasks. Think about what success requires and drive toward it."

8. "Anticipate needs and prepare for upcoming phases rather than reacting only when you arrive at each step."

9. "You're authorized to make decisions on routine matters within [scope]—you don't need approval for every action."

10. "This pattern of waiting for direction on straightforward work is a performance concern. I need to see more independent, proactive engagement going forward."

SUMMARY: PERFORMANCE & COMPETENCE

THE FIVE CONVERSATIONS YOU JUST GOT THROUGH

So you've made it through the worst of it—the five performance conversations that keep managers up at night. The ones where you have to tell someone their work isn't cutting it, they're too slow, they don't understand something everyone else grasped immediately, they can't manage a calendar, or they need you to direct every single move they make.

Fun times, right?

Here's what we just covered:

Chapter 1: When Work Quality Is Below Standard - How to say "this is terrible" without actually saying those words. Because sometimes work is just objectively bad, and pretending otherwise helps no one.

Chapter 2: Addressing Slow Workers & Low Productivity - How to tell someone they're painfully slow without getting accused of creating a pressure cooker environment. When everyone else finishes in two hours and they need two days, somebody has to say something.

Chapter 3: When They Don't Get It (Comprehension Issues) - The most frustrating conversation of all: explaining something for the fifth time and watching them still not understand it. How to address comprehension gaps without saying "are you dense?"

Chapter 4: Missed Deadlines & Poor Time Management - Handling the employee who treats deadlines as decorative suggestions. How to require actual delivery without sounding unreasonable.

Chapter 5: Lack of Initiative & Passive Work Styles - Dealing with someone who does exactly what's asked and not one thing more. How to say "think for yourself" in language that won't land you in HR.

WHAT THESE CONVERSATIONS HAVE IN COMMON

If you paid attention (and if you've gotten this far, you probably did), you noticed some patterns:

Get Specific or Get Nowhere

"You need to do better" accomplishes exactly nothing. "Your last three reports had calculation errors that required rework" is something someone can actually address. Vague feedback is cowardly feedback disguised as kindness.

Not Every Problem Needs the Nuclear Option

First time someone misses a deadline? Diplomatic approach. Fifth time? Firm conversation with consequences. The escalation matters. Don't bring a flamethrower to a conversation that needs a match, and don't bring a match to a conversation that needs a flamethrower.

Your Words Create Your Paper Trail

Notice how the phrases include documentation language naturally? "We've discussed this multiple times," "This is the third instance," "I need to see improvement within two weeks." You're building the record while having the conversation. That's not an accident.

Effort Doesn't Trump Results

Someone can work really hard and still produce garbage. Someone can seem busy all day and produce nothing. The conversations in these chapters focus on what actually gets delivered, not how much someone appears to be trying. Because at the end of the day, results matter more than sweat equity.

Clarity Is Kindness

The cruelest thing you can do is let someone think everything's fine when it's not. Sugarcoating until your words are meaningless doesn't help anyone—it just delays the inevitable harder conversation. Being clear enough that they understand the problem while being professional enough that you're not a jerk? That's the goal.

WHY THESE PHRASES WORK

The language in these five chapters isn't magic. It works because:

It's Honest Without Being Brutal

There's a massive difference between "your work isn't meeting standards" and "you're incompetent." One addresses the problem. The other attacks the person. The phrases throughout this section live in that gap—direct enough to be meaningful, diplomatic enough to be professional.

It Focuses on What You Can See

Instead of mind-reading or character assassination, the language targets observable, demonstrable issues. "You're asking questions about things we covered in the same conversation" is a fact. "You don't listen" is an accusation. See the difference?

It Doesn't Just Complain—It Sets Direction

Nearly every scenario includes not just "this is wrong" but "here's what needs to change." You're not just dumping criticism on someone and walking away. You're establishing expectations for improvement.

It Keeps You Out of Trouble

The phrases avoid the kind of language that gets managers called into HR. No assumptions about motivation. No attacks on intelligence. No accusations you can't prove. Just observable gaps between what's expected and what's delivered.

The Reality Nobody Talks About

Here's the uncomfortable truth: not everyone can do every job. Sometimes the comprehension gap is too large. Sometimes the skill ceiling is too low. Sometimes the speed will never match what the position requires.

That's not your fault as a manager. Your job isn't to turn every employee into a star performer through sheer force of will and perfect phrasing. Your job is to:

1. Be clear about what's not working
2. Set explicit expectations for improvement
3. Give reasonable opportunity to get better
4. Document what happens next

Sometimes these conversations lead to dramatic improvement. Sometimes they lead to someone finding a role better suited to their abilities. Both outcomes are fine. What's not fine is avoiding the conversation entirely and hoping things magically improve.

You Can't Want Their Success More Than They Do

You can provide crystal-clear feedback. You can offer resources. You can set consequences. But at the end of the day, improvement is on them. Your responsibility is clarity about what's needed. Their responsibility is delivering it.

If they choose not to—or can't—that's on them, not you.

The Conversation Is Just the Start

Having the talk matters, but what happens afterward matters more. Are you following up? Acknowledging improvement? Documenting continued issues? The phrases in this book open the door. You still have to walk through it with actual accountability.

BEFORE YOUR NEXT PERFORMANCE CONVERSATION

Figure out which problem you're actually addressing. Don't lump "they're slow AND the work is bad AND they don't get it" into one conversation. Pick the primary issue. Use the relevant chapter. Focus.

Get specific examples ready. "Your work has been problematic" gets you nowhere. "The last three reports had errors that required significant rework, costing the team six hours" is something you can discuss.

Match your tone to the situation. First time? Go diplomatic. Third time discussing the same problem? Time to be firm. The escalation levels in each scenario exist for a reason.

Pick phrases that sound like you. Find 2-3 options from the chapter that feel natural to your style. Adapt them. Practice saying them out loud (yes, really). Stumbling through a script you hate helps no one.

Know what comes next. What improvement do you need? By when? How will you track it? The conversation should end with clarity, not ambiguity.

AFTER THE CONVERSATION

Document it. Send a follow-up email: "As we discussed, I need to see [specific change] by [timeframe]." Keep it factual. File it. Move on.

Actually follow through. If you said you'd check in weekly, do it. If you set a deadline, track it. Empty threats destroy your credibility faster than anything else.

Acknowledge improvement when it happens. If things get better, say so. "The last two reports were solid—keep it up" takes five seconds and reinforces progress.

Escalate when nothing changes. If the same problem continues after multiple clear conversations, involve HR. You've done your part. Now it's time for the professionals.

THE BOTTOM LINE

These five conversations are uncomfortable because you're essentially telling someone they're failing at something they're supposed to be able to do. That sucks for everyone involved.

But avoiding these conversations doesn't help:

- It doesn't help them (they deserve to know where they stand)
- It doesn't help the team (who's affected by their performance)
- It doesn't help you (who's stuck managing around their limitations)
- It doesn't help the organization (which needs capable people in critical roles)

Being a good manager doesn't mean being everyone's friend. It means having the spine to address problems clearly while maintaining some basic human decency. You can be direct without being an asshole. You can be honest without being cruel. You can hold people accountable without being unreasonable.

The phrases in these five chapters give you the language to do that.

WHAT'S COMING NEXT

This book covered the five most common performance and competence conversations—when work quality is subpar, productivity is low, comprehension is lacking, deadlines are missed, and initiative is absent.

But managing people involves more than just performance issues.

What about the employee who's technically competent but insufferable to work with? The one who's checked out and phoning it in? The person who's unreliable, makes terrible decisions, or is just fundamentally unprofessional?

Those conversations require different language, and they're covered in the companion volumes:

- **HR Approved Ways To Tell Employees (Almost) Anything: Behavior & Professionalism Edition**
- **HR Approved Ways To Tell Employees (Almost) Anything: Workplace Situations Edition**

Each book in the series follows the same principle: direct enough to matter, diplomatic enough to survive.

And if you need to handle difficult colleagues as a peer, not a manager, check out where it all started: **HR Approved Ways To Say (Almost) Anything To Coworkers** with 500+ tips for navigating workplace relationships without the power dynamic.

Visit **https://hrapprovedways.com/** for the complete series, downloadable phrase cards, video demonstrations, and a community of managers who actually get it.

So, the next time you're facing a performance conversation, you have the language you need.

Go have that talk you've been avoiding.

And remember: the kindest thing you can do for someone who's underperforming is tell them the truth. They might hate hearing it, but clarity beats false hope every single time.

The conversations are hard. The language doesn't have to be.

If this book gave you the language to finally have that conversation you'd been avoiding, other managers need to know about it.

Most managers are lying awake at 2 am, wondering how to tell someone their work isn't good enough without getting called into HR. They're avoiding necessary conversations because nobody taught them what to actually say.

You found this book. They haven't yet.

A two-minute review helps other managers discover these tools when they need them most.

Scan the QR code below to leave your Amazon review, or visit the book's Amazon page directly.

Reviews that help other managers most often share:

- Which conversation were you dreading
- Whether the phrases worked for your situation
- If you actually used the language (and what happened)

You don't need to write an essay. Even "Finally, actual words I could use for [situation]" helps.

Thanks for being the kind of manager who cares enough to do this right. And if you leave a review? You're helping another manager find the words they desperately need.

—The HR Approved Ways Team

CONTINUE YOUR JOURNEY: THE COMPLETE HR APPROVED WAYS SERIES

YOU'VE MASTERED PERFORMANCE CONVERSATIONS—NOW WHAT?

This book gave you the language for the five most common performance and competence conversations. But let's be honest: performance issues are only part of what makes management exhausting.

What about the employee who's technically competent but so abrasive that everyone avoids working with them? The one who's clearly checked out and phoning it in? The person who's unreliable, unprofessional, or just... difficult?

Those conversations require different language—and fortunately, we've got you covered.

PART II: BEHAVIOR & PROFESSIONALISM

"HR Approved Ways To Tell Employees (Almost) Anything: Behavior & Professionalism Edition"

This companion volume tackles the conversations that happen when someone can do the work, but their behavior is the problem:

- **Chapter 1: Interpersonal Problems & Poor People Skills** - "Let's Work on Communication Style" (Translation: People Can't Stand Working With You)
- **Chapter 2: Attitude & Effort Issues** - "I Need to See More Engagement" (Translation: You Clearly Don't Care)
- **Chapter 3: Reliability & Follow-Through Problems** - "I Need Consistency From You" (Translation: I Can't Trust You to Do Your Job)
- **Chapter 4: Professional Judgment & Decision-Making** - "Let's Review Your Approach" (Translation: That Was a Dumb Decision)

Because sometimes the work itself is fine—the person doing it is the problem.

PART III: SPECIFIC WORKPLACE SITUATIONS

"HR Approved Ways To Tell Employees (Almost) Anything: Workplace Situations Edition"

This volume handles the specific, situational conversations that don't fit neatly into performance or behavior categories:

- **Chapter 1: Mistakes, Errors & Preventable Problems** - "Let's Discuss What Happened" (Translation: You Screwed Up)
- **Chapter 2: Communication Failures** - "We Need to Improve Information Sharing" (Translation: You Don't Communicate Effectively)
- **Chapter 3: Meeting & Collaboration Problems** - "Let's Review Meeting Expectations" (Translation: You're Wasting Everyone's Time)
- **Chapter 4: Remote Work Performance Issues** - "Let's Align on Remote Work Standards" (Translation: I Know You're Not Really Working)

- **Chapter 5: Skills Gaps & Capability Limits** - "Let's Discuss Development Opportunities" (Translation: You're Not Qualified for This)
- **Chapter 6: The Performance Conversation Roadmap** - Building Your Case: From First Talk to Final Warning

The situations that make you think "there has to be a better way to say this"—there is, and it's in here.

WHERE IT ALL STARTED: THE PEER-TO-PEER GUIDE

"HR Approved Ways To Say (Almost) Anything To Coworkers"

500+ Tips On How to Talk to Anyone at Work, Master Workplace Communication With Humor Even With Difficult People

Before you were a manager, you were a coworker. And coworker dynamics operate under completely different rules because there's no power dynamic in play. This is the book that started it all—the peer-to-peer communication guide for:

- Setting boundaries with colleagues who overstep
- Addressing annoying behaviors without creating enemies
- Navigating office politics when everyone's on the same level
- Saying no without burning bridges
- Handling the colleague who talks too much, the one who steals credit, the one who's perpetually negative

If you manage people who also have to work with each other (spoiler: you do), this book helps them navigate those relationships without dragging you into every minor conflict.

GET THE COMPLETE COLLECTION

Each book in the HR Approved Ways series follows the same philosophy: **Be direct enough to create change, diplomatic enough to avoid disaster.**

Whether you're managing down, collaborating sideways, or navigating up, the language matters. These books give you the exact words to use when you know what needs to be said but can't figure out how to say it without causing a disaster.

VISIT US ONLINE

https://www.hrapprovedways.com/

At our website, you'll find:

- **The complete book series** with options for print, digital, and audio formats
- **Downloadable phrase cards** organized by situation—print them, keep them handy, use them
- **Video demonstrations** of difficult conversations (because sometimes seeing it helps more than reading it)
- **Monthly scenario discussions** where we tackle real situations submitted by readers
- **The Manager's Toolkit** with templates, checklists, and decision trees
- **A private community forum** where managers share their challenges and get real-world advice

Because let's be honest: reading about difficult conversations helps. Having a community of people who get it helps more.

WHICH BOOK DO YOU NEED RIGHT NOW?

If you're dealing with someone whose work is subpar:

You just finished the right book. Use it.

If the work is fine but the person is insufferable, checked out, or unprofessional:

You need the Behavior & Professionalism edition.

If you're facing a specific situation like a major screw-up, communication breakdown, or capability crisis:

Grab the Workplace Situations edition.

If you're not a manager yet but need to survive working with difficult colleagues:

Start with the original Coworkers edition—it's where this whole thing began.

If you're a manager who wants the complete toolkit:

Get all three management editions. Because problems don't arrive in neat categories, and neither should your solutions.

ONE MORE THING

These books exist because managing people is hard and nobody teaches you the actual words to say when conversations get uncomfortable. There isn't a school that covers "how to tell someone they're slow without getting sued." Leadership training doesn't give you the exact phrasing for "your work is consistently terrible."

We do.

You're not alone in finding these conversations difficult. You're not the only one replaying conversations in your head, searching for a way to be direct without losing your team's trust. And you're not the only one who wishes this part of being a manager came with a script.

That's what we're here for.

Visit https://hrapprovedways.com/ for resources that give you the language you need for every difficult conversation you're avoiding.

Because the conversations are hard enough, but communication doesn't have to be.

www.ingramcontent.com/pod-product-compliance
Lightning Source LLC
Chambersburg PA
CBHW071428130726
47997CB00006B/2002
9798992767940